Discover Newport's
Island
Cemetery

NOTABLE PEOPLE AND MONUMENTS
FROM THE GILDED AGE TO MODERN TIMES

Discover Newport's

Island

Cemetery

NOTABLE PEOPLE AND MONUMENTS
FROM THE GILDED AGE TO MODERN TIMES

Trudy and Lewis Keen
for the benefit of the Friends of Island Cemetery

Front cover: Belmont Circle featuring the exedra. *Photo by the author.*
Back cover: Belmont Circle featuring the chapel. *Photo by the author.*

Published by Ingram Sparks
Https://www.ingramspark.com

Book Layout ©2023 BookDesignTemplates.com

Discover Newport's Island Cemetery: Notable People and Monuments from the Gilded Age to Modern Times/ Trudy and Lew Keen. —1st ed.3

ISBN 979-8-218-19708-7

Contents

About this book

This book was created to allow the reader to engage in themed, self-guided tours of Island Cemetery located in Newport, Rhode Island. Each chapter, or tour, begins with a map indicating the location of the people or gravestones included for that particular theme. Some individuals are included in more than one tour, and the information shared may vary based on the theme. To read all the information about a person, consult the index.

At the end of the book is a map showing all the noted grave locations followed by a listing of the people included. A grid has been applied to the map to make grave location easier. To fit the initials for each grave onto the exact grave site would have made the map unreadable, so the text is enlarged beyond the lot boundaries. The locations indicated on the map are approximate but close enough to make finding stones easy. Photographs of many of the stones appear on the Rhode Island Cemetery Database (http://rihistoriccemeteries.org). The photographs may help locate a specific stone or grave.

Selecting "notable" people is a subjective task. For centuries, society has honored military heroes and politicians with statues and gravesite ceremonies. This book strives to expand the notables to include a more varied reflection of modern times and its people. While Island Cemetery is the final resting place of wealthy and famous people, it is also the site where many middle class Newporters were laid to rest. Their stories are equally worthy of note. Future exploration into the people buried in Island Cemetery will certainly yield additional notable people to celebrate.

All proceeds from the sale of this publication will go directly to the Friends of Island Cemetery for preservation of this historic site.

We would like to thank Pam Kelley, Sharon Hussey, Betsey Oestreich and Zach Russell for their encouragement and assistance with this project. Thanks also to Stephen Iwanski at Charter Books for his guidance with formatting this publication.

Cedar Way was added to the cemetery in 2022 as a final resting place for cremains.

CHAPTER ONE

Introductory Tour of Island Cemetery

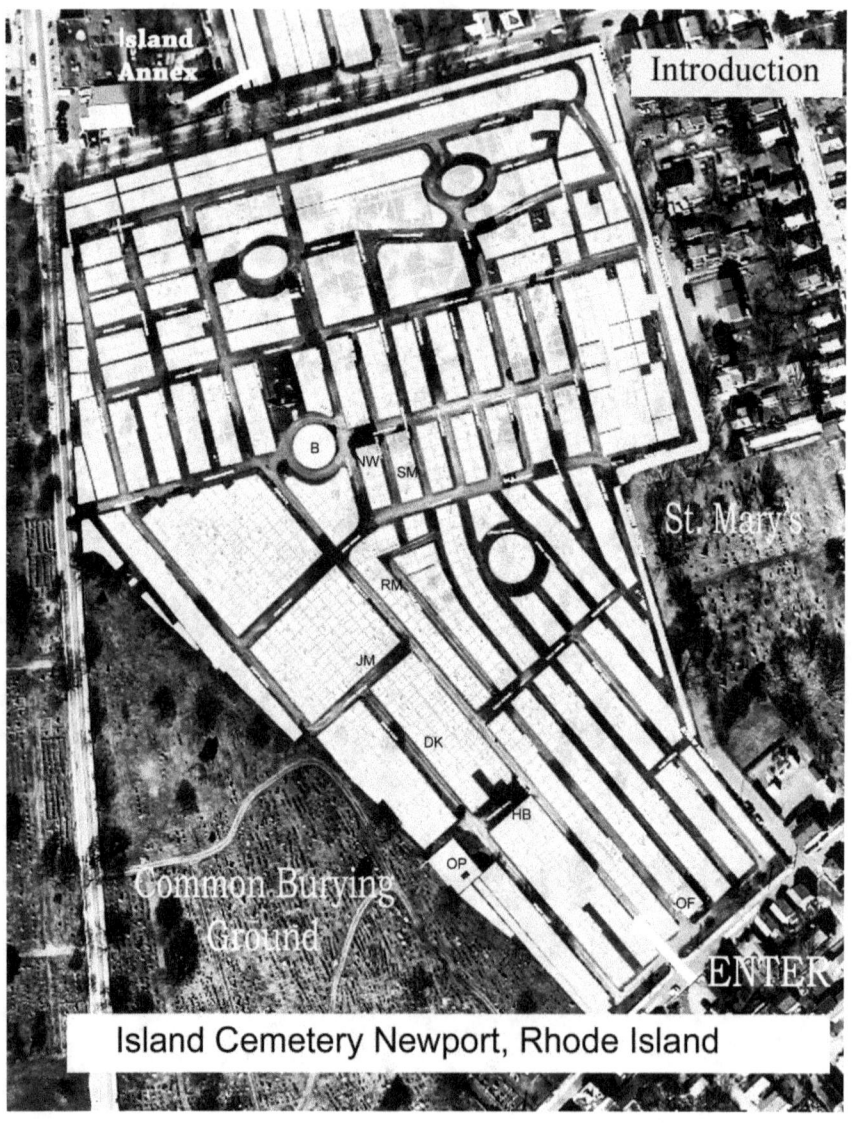

Island Annex

Introduction

St. Mary's

B
NW
SM
RM
JM
DK
HB
OP
OF

Common Burying Ground

ENTER

Island Cemetery Newport, Rhode Island

The Rural Cemetery

At the entrance to Island Cemetery

The Industrial Revolution began in Britain in the 1830s and came soon after to the United States. The introduction of steam power mechanized many industries and drew people from farms to cities, and those cities were soon overcrowded with the living and the dead. Burial grounds were usually within the confines of the city or in city churchyards. In some major European cities, graves were used over and over again, and in some places, people were buried four deep in one grave. The use of coffins and embalming was not a widespread practice at the time, and decaying corpses were causing health issues for the living.

In Paris in 1804, Napoleon issued a decree governing all future internments. Burials had to be 40-50 yards beyond the city limits, no mass burials were permitted, and there had to be a certain distance between bodies. Cemeteries had to be elevated and preferably exposed to the north wind. Trees had to be planted to absorb miasma, the poisonous air that resulted from decaying bodies.[1] This decree resulted in the first large rural cemetery in the world.

The City of Paris purchased the elevated 48-acre estate of a Jesuit priest known as Pere la Chaise. There was some resistance to burials there at first among the upper class because many wanted to be buried on their own estates while others avoided the site because it was in the 20th arrondissement, far from the city center. Initially trees and shrubs dominated the site, but as the popularity of the site increased, more monuments appeared and plantings disappeared.[2]

The creation of Pere la Chaise inspired some in the City of Boston to establish their own rural cemetery. The idea was proposed by medical doctor, Jacob Bigelow, and heavily supported by the Massachusetts Horticultural Society. Initially the city acquired 70 acres which overlooked the Charles River and provided panoramic views of the surrounding area.[3] The plans for the layout included roads wide enough to accommodate hearses and large water features.[4] Philadelphia followed suit with Laurel Hill Cemetery in 1834, and New York opened their garden cemetery, Greenwood, in Brooklyn in 1838. All three offered beautifully landscaped grounds and different elevations. The garden cemetery was the impetus for the public park system in American cities and established the profession of landscape gardening throughout the United States.[5]

---

[1] James R. Cothran and Erica Danylchak, *Grave Landscapes: The Nineteenth Century Rural Cemetery Movement* (Columbia, South Carolina: The University of South Carolina Press, 2018), 33.

[2] Cothran and Danylchak, 34.

[3] Joy M. Giguere, *Characteristically American: Memorial Architecture, National Identity, and the Egyptian Revival* (Knoxville, Tennessee: The University of Tennessee Press, 2014), 53-55.

[4] Cothran and Danylchak, 39-45.

[5] Cothran and Danylchak, xiii.

The rural cemetery movement coincided with and was spurred on by a changing attitude toward death. The European Romantic Movement led to Transcendentalism in New England, which emphasized the importance of nature. Changing attitudes toward death also occurred, and the old boneyard or graveyard became known as a cemetery, from the Greek word meaning "sleeping place." Burial sites went from places to be feared to places where one could visit the grave of a loved one while enjoying the serenity of nature.[6]

Island Cemetery is a fraction of the size of the average large city rural cemetery and has a flat topography, but Newport was and still is a small city in comparison.

The Creation of Island Cemetery

map HB

According to city records, the City of Newport purchased land northeast of the Common Burying Ground in 1836, and with the assistance of Henry Bull and William W. Freeborn, the city's garden cemetery was planned. The city sold its remaining lots in the site to the other plot owners on December 23, 1847. The transaction was recorded April 12, 1848,[7] and the site was incorporated under the name Island Cemetery Company. The initial trustees were David King, Henry Cranston, William Stevens, Henry Bull, Joseph Weaver, Benjamin Marsh Jr., and Henry H. Cook.

---

[6] Cothran and Danylchak, 37.

[7] December 23, 1847 between town treasurer George Freeborn and William Stevens, Michael Freeborn, Benjamin Marsh and Henry Cook- committee of the proprietors of the new burial site. City of Newport Property Records.

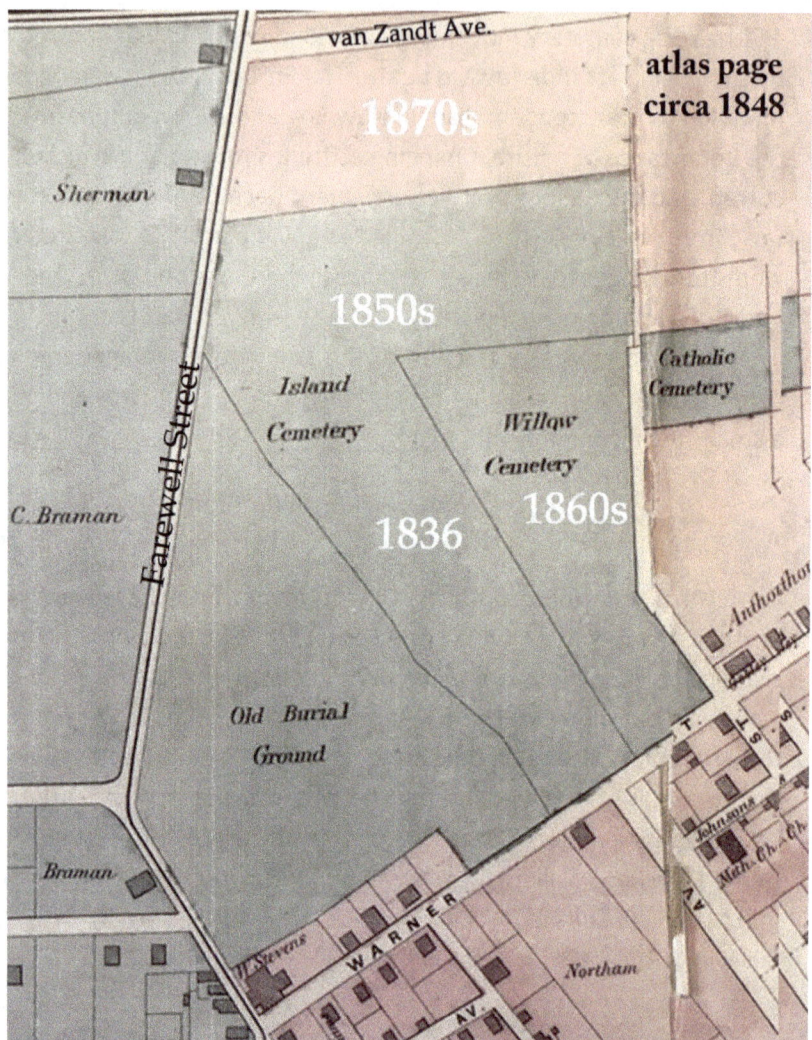

Additional land was added to the original acreage three times in the 1850s. In 1850, an acre was purchased from Elijah Sherman for $600. It was part of the Townsend lot, east of the Common Burying Ground and north of the original Island Cemetery land. In 1855 the company purchased a second parcel from Elijah Sherman that had also been part of the Townsend lot. For $1467.38 they obtained 1.25 acres of land, and it too sat east of the Common Burying Ground and adjacent to the Island Cemetery property. Finally in 1858 the company purchased from Elijah Sherman for $2328, "4 acres and 2 rods, 25 rods, and 51 feet" of land. This land was adjacent to the Willow Cemetery and east of the Island Cemetery.

In 1866 four transactions allowed Island Cemetery to add the adjacent Willow Cemetery (established 1851) to its holdings. The final parcel of land was purchased in the 1870s from Charles Spooner and Lewis Simmons and was along the current Van Zandt Avenue. This purchase completed the cemetery as it exists today.

One of the men involved in the cemetery from the beginning was Henry Bull (1815-1899). He was the sixth Henry

in Newport and a direct descendant of the first Henry Bull, a founding member of the city in 1639. Bull was a prominent businessman in Newport and was the second president of the Island Cemetery Company. His vast real estate holdings in the city included the Opera House and the Perry House. His son, Melville Bull, was a U.S. Representative and his son, William Bull, was a respected doctor.

Oliver Hazard Perry

map OP

Perhaps more distinguished than the Bull family was the Perry family. Christopher Raymond Perry (1761-1818) was a captain in the United States Navy. His youngest son, Matthew Calbraith Perry (1794-1858), rose to the rank of commodore in the Navy and is best known for opening trade with Japan in 1858. The older Perry son, Oliver Hazard Perry (1785-1819), was the most well-known of the family. He was born in South Kingston, Rhode Island, first served in the Navy in 1799 under the command of his  father and was assigned his first ship command in 1809. He earned fame in 1813 when he led the American forces to victory over the British in the Battle of Lake Erie in the War of 1812. "We have met the enemy and he is ours," is his most well-known quote. While serving the country on a diplomatic mission to Venezuela in 1819, Perry contracted yellow fever and died. Originally buried in Port Spain, Trinidad, his body was returned to Newport in 1826 and buried in the Common Burying Ground. His remains were relocated once again in 1841 to a square of land in the Common Burying Ground that had been purchased by the state with plans to erect a fitting monument to this naval hero.

Visit the Perry monument today and you will notice it is in the Island Cemetery, not the Common Burying Ground, but close to the border of the two sites. A careful examination of atlas pages during this time and a visual inspection of the existing boundary line between the two sites leads one to the conclusion that the boundary line was adjusted to include Perry in the Island Cemetery. Sources confirm that the line shifted in 1843,[8] and it is likely a powerful person like Henry Bull, would have been instrumental in the effort to make the change. In 1828 Henry Bull was one of the men appointed by the state to establish a monument for Perry. In 1843 the city still owned part of the Island Cemetery, so a shift of boundary between the two sites was not an important issue. The inclusion of Perry in the newer site would be a good selling point for unsold lots since famous burials in a site were good for business.

The trustees of the Island Cemetery continued to buy additional land in the 20th century that was not contiguous to the existing site. 79 acres purchased near the harbor in 1920 were taken in 1940 by the United States Navy for their base. The Island Cemetery Annex currently on Van Zandt Avenue was purchased in August of 1926 from Arendt Brandt. One additional land purchase of note that took place in 1932 was the Society of Friends site located a few blocks from the main cemetery.

---

[8] Https://www.islandcemeterynewport.com.

The Belmont Chapel

map B

In addition to land purchases, the site was improved with structures and fencing. Starting in 1886, the Belmont Memorial Chapel was built. The chapel was gifted for use at the cemetery by August Belmont in memory of his daughter, Jane Pauline Belmont, who was 19 years old when she died in 1875. The firm of George C. Mason and Son designed the chapel in the Gothic style and it was built by William Gosling,[9] who built the Armory on Thames Street[10] in 1894, currently home to the Sailing Museum. Gosling is listed in Newport City Directories as a mason or stone worker. The chapel and furnishing designs are attributed to George Champlin Mason Jr. [11]

---

[9] Belmont Chapel Foundation website. Https://belmontchapelfoundation.org/chapel-history/

[10] Southern Thames Historic District National Register of Historic Places Registration Form, 2008. Https://preservation.ri.gov/sites/g/files/xkg-bur406/files/pdfs_zips_downloads/national_pdfs/newport/newp_southern-thames-hd.pdf.

[11] Ron Onorato, "An Architect and His Environment: The Career of George Champlin Mason Jr." *Newport History*; *Journal of the Newport Historical Society,* Vol. 91 (Summer/Fall 2019), No. 280, 29.

The following is a Chapel description from an August 20, 1887 news article:

The Belmont Chapel, Interesting Description of the Beautiful Altar and Elegant Furnishings

The Belmont Memorial Chapel is completed, so far as relates to the structure, but one after another beautiful feature has been added to the interior, and of these the most striking is the altar, recently placed in the chapel– an exquisite work of art that is the admiration of every one of who has been so fortunate as to see it. It is seven feet in length and is composed of Caen stone and different marbles with onyx columns, the latter polished like gems. The center panel bears the sacred monogram, in each of the others there is a cross in relief, and over all are vines delicately carved and tenderly clinging to every point that offers support– cut by hands that realized how beautiful they are and how appropriately used for ornamentation. The corners of the altar are supported by life-size kneeling cherubs, whose flowing robes and graceful wings blend in and make a part of the structure, their hands clasped upon their breasts, and their eyes raised heavenward with a look of love and adoration.

On the super-alter of marble there is this inscription: This Chapel Erected

to the Glory of God and in memory of Jane Pauline Belmont. Resting upon the super-altar there is a low cross, of the purest statuary marble, adorned with a wreath of flowers that cling around the word "Patience," cut in relief upon the arms of the cross. This cross was taken from over the grave of Miss Belmont and upon its base is handsomely carved the following: Jane Pauline Belmont, Born April 11, 1856, Died October 15th 1875.

Belmont Chapel Pew detail- The whole is a study, and we are not surprised that many persons, hearing of it, have been attracted to the spot. Another recent feature is the chancel rail, of floriated and highly polished hammered brass, resting upon a sculptured base of Caen stone, over and around which ivies cling, cut by the same hands that so faithfully carried out the design for the altar. The benches in the nave are of oak, each bench having its own design. On one the oak is introduced, on another, the fern, then the wild roses, the hawthorn, and so on; no two being alike. The designs of these beautiful features were furnished by Mr. George C. Mason,  *Jr. under whose supervision they have been brought to perfection. The altar and other stone work was executed by Mr. Robert D. Kelley of Philadelphia; the brass work by the Joseph Newmann co. also of Philadelphia, and the benches by Mr. Thomas S. Nason, of this city.*[12]

In 2014 a nonprofit organization was formed to restore the Belmont Chapel under the leadership of Harry Eudenbach. The organization also included Robert Currier, Lois McCormick, Peter Booth, Robert Vitello and Abigail Campbell-King.

---

[12] "The Belmont Memorial Chapel," *Newport Mercury*, (20 August 1887), 1.

19th Century Monuments

Island Cemetery features monuments and gravestones of great variety in design and material. Slate ledger and tablet head stones and foot stones were the most common grave markers in the 1700s, and Island Cemetery has a few within its borders. The majority of gravestones in Island Cemetery, however, are either marble or granite. Marble is the older material used and most often as tablet stones (without foot stones) or obelisks. Ancient Egyptians were regarded as the great caretakers of the dead,[13] and the obelisk, borrowed from their culture, became ubiquitous in American cemeteries. The Oliver Hazard Perry monument is a good example of an obelisk. The Samuel Marsh monument (later in this tour) displays Egyptian features in a different form and has a winged orb with serpent. The Perry family marble tablet stones that surround the obelisk are the most common forms of grave markers for much of the 1800s.

map DK

The marble monument for Dr. David King (1774-1836) is an example of a false sarcophagus that was popular in the last quarter of the 19th century.[14] Dr. King was one of the first burials in Island Cemetery, and the sarcophagus was added later by one or more of his sons since two of Dr. King's sons made vast fortunes in the China Trade. The false sarcophagus is called

---

[13] Giguere, *Characteristically American*, 7.

[14] Richard Francis Veit, *New Jersey Cemeteries and Tombstones: History in the Landscape.* (New Brunswick, New Jersey: Rutgers University Press/Rivergate Books, 2008), 169.

that since the body of the deceased is buried in the ground and not entombed in the sarcophagus.

The sarcophagus, which often has feet to give it more height and grandeur, is highly ornamented with winged cherubs signifying the carrying of the soul to heaven. On the back is a poppy stem which signifies deep sleep.

Dr. King is credited with giving the first smallpox inoculation in the state of Rhode Island and for his support of the Rhode Island Medical Society. He is also credited with reinvigorating interest in the Redwood Library and served as its president from 1830 until his death in 1836.[15]

In the same plot is the grave of Dr. King's oldest son, George Gordon King, who served in the United States House of Representatives from 1849-1853. His marble box tomb is placed over the grave and does not contain his body. Next to the tomb is a stone very typical of the mid-Victorian era for Mr. King's wife and infant daughter, who both died in 1853.

The flowers on the stone signify the brevity of life.[16] This is particularly appropriate since Mrs. King died at 27 and her daughter at less than one year of age. The garland seems to be made of roses, symbolizing purity, and morning glories, symbolizing resurrection.[17]

Other civilizations that America looked to for inspiration were the Greek and Roman. In both cultures many practiced the rite of

---

[15] Collection of the Redwood Library and Athenaeum, Newport, Rhode Island.

[16] Jessie Lie Farber, *Symbolism in the Carvings on Old Gravestones* (Greenfield, Massachusetts: The Association for Gravestone Studies, 1986), 2.

[17] Douglas Keister, *Stories in Stone: A Field Guide to Cemetery Symbolism and Iconography* (Salt Lake City, Utah: Gibbs Smith, 2004), 50,53.

cremation, and the ashes of the deceased were put into urns. Even after burials became preferrable, the urn remained closely associated with cemeteries. The drape over the urn became popular with the drape representing the barrier between earth and heaven or between life and death.[18]

map JM

George Munro's stone contains ivy, which can survive in the harshest atmosphere and is associated with immortality and steadfastness. Because of the three-pointed leaf, it is also symbolic of the Holy Trinity.[19] The fern on Elizabeth Munro's stone symbolizes humility and sincerity[20] since ferns grow deep in the forest and can be found only by someone who has honestly searched for them. The same can be said for people of great faith. On the stones of William J. Munro and his wife, oak leaves depict strength and faith,[21] and bulrushes on each stone represent salvation or being saved, as Moses was from the Nile River.[22]

---

[18] Cothran and Danylchak, 174.

[19] Keister, 57.

[20] Keister, 47.

[21] Keister, 62.

[22] Amanda Norman and Mark Kneale, "A to Z of Headstone Symbols|Headstone Symbols and Meanings" (2 September 2017). Https://headstonesymbols.co.uk/

map B

Commodore Matthew Perry, a Newport native, was the father of August Belmont's wife Jane. He is remembered for his brilliant naval career during which he commanded ships in the War of 1812 and in the Mexican-American War.

What really put him in the history books was his campaign on behalf of our nation to open Japan to trade with the Western world. [23]

When he died in 1858, the family wanted to honor his request for burial in Newport, but the weather prevented them from doing so. Instead, Perry was buried in his wife's family's vault in St. Mark's-in-the-Bowerie Church in New York City. In 1866 at the request of his wife and daughter, his remains were disinterred and reburied in the Belmont plot in Island Cemetery close to his parents' graves. In 1873 his widow Jane erected a highly decorated false sarcophagus over his grave.[24]

The sarcophagus is decorated with laurel wreaths, the Greek decoration for heroes, olive branches for peace, and a doe's head, a symbol taken from the Perry family crest.[25]

---

[23] Rockwell Stensrud, *Newport: A Lively Experiment* (Newport, Rhode Island: The Redwood Library and Athenaeum, 2006), 313.

[24] Find a Grave, database and images (https://www.findagrave.com/memorial/804/matthew-calbraith-perry: accessed 16 July 2021), memorial page for Matthew Calbraith Perry (10 Apr 1794–4 Mar 1858), Find a Grave Memorial ID 804, citing Island Cemetery, Newport, Newport County, Rhode Island, USA; Maintained by Find A Grave.

[25] "Monument to Commodore M.C. Perry." *New York Times* (15 August 1873), https://www.newyorktimes.com.

Perry's family commissioned sculptor John Quincy Adams Ward to create a life-size statue of M.C. Perry that was erected in Touro Park in 1869. The base for the statue was designed by Richard Morris Hunt and commemorates Perry's life with scenes of his accomplishments.[26]

August Belmont was born in Germany in 1816 and, through a family member, got a job as an errand boy with the Rothschilds Bank.

They were impressed with his work ethic, and he soon became a private secretary to one of the brothers.[27]

In 1837 he was sent to Cuba to protect the Rothschilds' interests during the Spanish Civil war. When Belmont arrived in New York, he found a bank panic in progress and noted that the agents representing the Rothschilds had closed their office. There was no time to ask for approval from his bosses since mail took weeks to arrive, so Belmont took it upon himself to open an office naming himself as the Rothschilds' agent. People trusted the name Rothschild so Belmont found himself doing business very quickly in New York. The Rothschilds were so pleased with Belmont's quick thinking to save their interests,

---

[26] Ronald J. Onorato and American Institute of Architects, Rhode Island Chapter. *AIA Guide to Newport* (Providence, Rhode Island: AIAri Architectural Forum, 2007), 136-137.

[27] David Black, *The King of Fifth Avenue: The Fortunes of August Belmont* (New York: The Dial Press, 1981), 15.

that they gave him a $10,000 a year salary, making him one of the richest men in New York by 1840.[28]

Belmont did not receive immediate social acceptance since he was a foreigner, but he dressed more lavishly than the old Knickerbocker families and had impeccable manners. After a few years, people began to take notice of him, and in the late 1840's Belmont met, and in 1849,

married Caroline Perry, the youngest daughter of Matthew Calbraith Perry.[29]

Belmont continued as a banker and got involved in national politics and horseracing. He had a lavish mansion at 109 Fifth Avenue. In 1860 the Belmonts spent a summer in Newport in a rented villa and so enjoyed themselves that they commissioned George Champlin Mason to build their summer home, Bythesea.[30]

Belmont is credited by biographer David Black as introducing Newport to the ten-course meal and informal dances. He also had an enormous staff employed at Bythesea.[31] In New York Belmont had a vast private art collection, which he loaned out once to raise money for the poor.[32] Several historians have also credited Belmont with starting the practice of driving up and down Bellevue Avenue to see and be seen.

Between 1851 and 1863, the Belmonts had six children. Their daughter Pauline had stomach problems from the time she was seven or eight, and those problems worsened as the years went on. During

---

[28] Black, 22-25, 39.
[29] Black, 60-68.
[30] Onorato, *AIA Guide,* 67.
[31] Black, 192.
[32] Black, 171-172.

the last few years of her life, she subsisted on milk and morphine, which was all her doctors could do for her.[33] Her grave marker is decorated with lilies and ivy, which represent purity and faith, but more telling is the word *patience* on the stone. She died at the age of 19 in 1875, and in her memory, Belmont commissioned George Champlin Mason to build a chapel near the family burial plot.[34]

Not long after construction of the chapel began in 1886, Belmont's son Raymond shot himself. Whether or not the shooting was an accident or suicide was never determined.[35]

Neither August nor Caroline Belmont ever quite recovered from the deaths of the two children who predeceased them. In addition, Belmont became increasingly concerned about financial matters, especially those involving his three remaining sons. His health in general began to fail, and in late November he came down with pneumonia and died on November 24, 1890, two weeks before his 77th birthday.

Perhaps the most exuberant marble monument in this lot is the exedra created for August and Caroline Belmont at the east end of the Belmont circle. The Greek Revival monument was designed by architect Richard Morris Hunt and the female figures (caryatids) were carved by Karl Bitter. The work was commissioned by Oliver Hazard Perry Belmont to honor his parents in 1890.[36]

Almost thirty years after August Belmont's death, August Belmont Jr. commissioned John Quincy Adams Ward to create a statue of his father. Ward's earlier sculpture of Matthew Calbraith Perry was his first commission, and the Belmont statue was his last. The Belmont statue was cast in bronze at the Gorham Factory in Providence, Rhode Island.

---

[33] Black, 425, 451.

[34] Onorato, *AIA Guide,* 67.

[35] Black, 699-700.

[36] Paul R. Baker, *Richard Morris Hunt* (Cambridge, Massachusetts: MIT Press, 1986), 314.

The statue was displayed originally at Belcourt, the estate of August Belmont's son, Oliver Hazard Perry Belmont, but when the property was sold in 1941, the family presented it to the City of Newport and the statue sat in Washington Square. When the square was renamed Eisenhower Park, Belmont's huge likeness was moved next to the Belmont Chapel in Island Cemetery and remained there until 1985. The Metropolitan Museum of Art requested use of the statue for its retrospective exhibit of the works of JQA Ward in 1985, and the statue stayed at the museum until 1995, when it returned to Newport. The bronze masterpiece now sits at the corner of Bellevue Avenue and Narragansett Avenue outside the headquarters of the Preservation Society of Newport County.[37]

20th century monuments

map NW

Miss Wilks was born and raised in Newport, Rhode Island and later became a teacher. According to United States Census data, she was a

teacher at a private school in Newport. In 1910 she lived at 130 Touro Street with two other teachers, and the building may have been the site of the school.[38]

The stone marking her gravesite is interesting because it is made of slate, a material much more associated with the colonial era. This stone, however, is a reflection of how times had changed since it is not decorated with religious iconography but with the tools of Miss

---

[37] Onorato, *AIA Guide,* 198-199.
[38] Https://www.*Ancestry.com.*

Wilks' profession. The tympanum, or top of the stone, shows a quill pen in an ink well, a book and a compass. The Latin motto included on the slate stone, "fidelis usque ad mortem," means faithful unto death.

Although there are some slate stones in the cemetery, the use of granite grave markers started late in the 1800s and is the most used material today. It exists in a variety of colors (grey, black, red) and can be shaped in a variety of forms. Due to their lack of simplicity, many granite monuments that resemble obelisks may best be referred to as monuments and not obelisks.

map RM

A very unique granite monument, a large book, was erected to commemorate the life of Rebecca Thorndike Marin, a member of one of the wealthiest Boston Brahmin families of the time period. Her grandfather, Israel Thorndike, started out with a pound in his pocket at age 10 and made a huge fortune in shipping that allowed him to almost singlehandedly finance the Industrial Revolution in New England. He left a fortune that today would be worth at least 60 million dollars.[39]

The Thorndike family vacationed in Newport from 1840 on, and it was here that Rebecca met a dashing young Naval lieutenant named Mathias Marin *(picture on the right)*. Rebecca's father, Augustus Thorndike, wanted his daughter to marry someone of her own class and

---

[39] Timothy H. Kistner, *Federalist Tycoon: The Life and Times of Israel Thorndike* (Lanham, Maryland: University Press of America, 2015),168-169.

forbid her to have anything to do with Lt. Marin. Against her father's wishes, Rebecca eloped with Marin in 1849, and they lived their life together in Newport.

When Augustus Thorndike died in 1858, his lengthy will spelled out his discontent with his daughter's marriage:

"And as my said daughter Rebecca eloped with and married the said Marin not only without my consent but contrary to my express injunctions, and under circumstances of great deception and after full notice from me of the consequences of such a step as now declared in this will, it is my intention that no part of my estate beyond the said annuity of four hundred dollars a year, shall in any event go to my said daughter or her issue."

He went on to forbid anyone receiving anything from the will to give any money to Rebecca or risk losing their part of the inheritance.[40]

Captain Marin purchased this house on Kay Street from George H. Calvert. The 1893 Newport Atlas states the owner as Rebecca Marin, and the street to the right of the house was not yet established. When created, the street was named Marin Street.

---

[40] "An Implacable Father—the Will of Augustus Thorndike," *New York Times* (24 December 1858), 8.

CHAPTER TWO

Architects and Real Estate Tycoons Tour

The word architect comes from the Greek and means "chief carpenter." Prior to the middle of the 19th century, America had no architects as we think of the term today. The earliest men who erected buildings simply copied or adapted the plans or drawings of others.

In Newport, Richard Munday, who is credited with the building of the Colony House and Trinity Church, actually used the plans of Christopher Wren, who designed the buildings for London after the Great Fire of 1666.[41]

---

[41] James Yarnall, *Newport through its Architecture: A History of Styles from Postmedieval to Postmodern* (Hanover, New Hampshire: University Press of New England, 2005), 10-16.

A few years later, Peter Harrison, who built the Redwood Library, Touro Synagogue and Brick Market, adapted his plans from his vast library of architectural books, many of them with the designs of Italian architect Andrea Palladio.[42]

In fact, most of the men we think of as the architects of the buildings in Newport prior to 1860 were master builders and stone masons.

---

[42] Yarnall, 16-22.

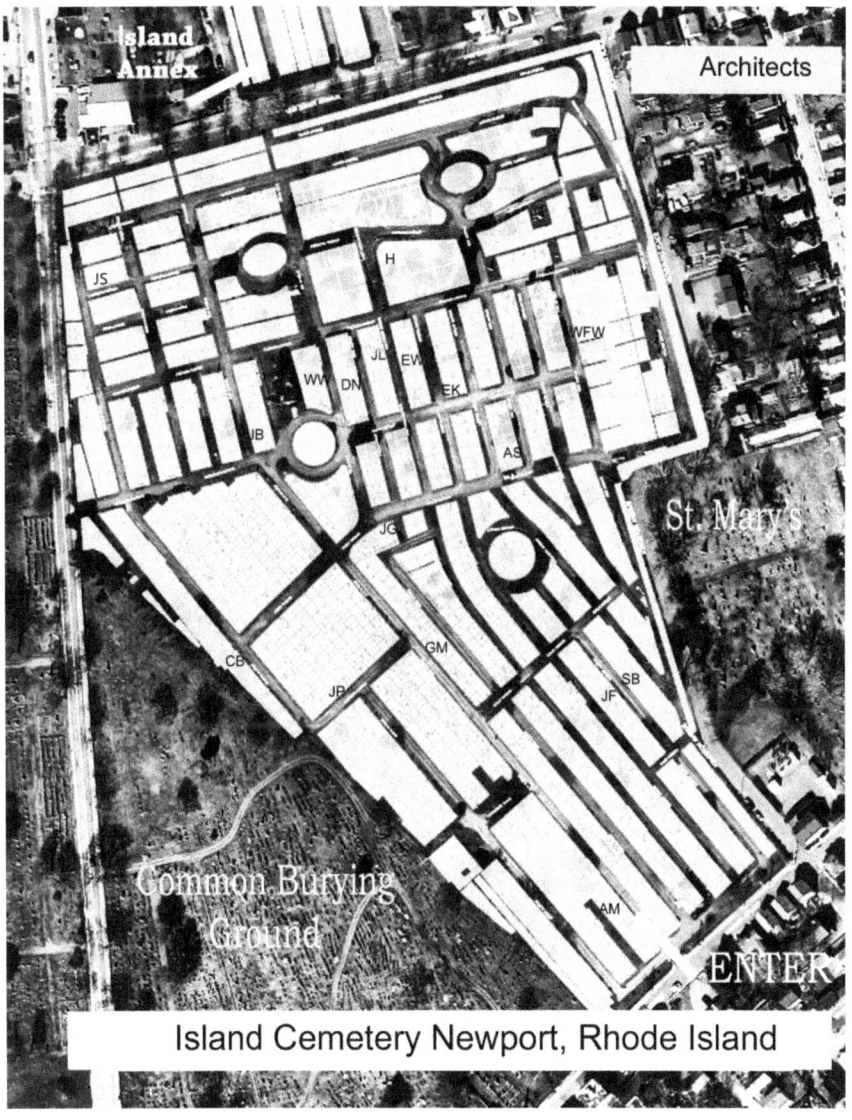

Island Cemetery Newport, Rhode Island

Joe Bailey

map JB

Joe Bailey (1802-1877) was member of a family that owned acreage in Newport for multiple generations. He is listed as a farmer in the 1850 census, a merchant in 1860 and a retired merchant in 1870. He was involved in buying and selling properties with Alfred Smith, and lived with his family at 20 Kay Street.[43]

Charles Lovatt Bevins

map CB

Bevins (1844-1925) was born in England and immigrated to the United States in 1878. He initially worked for Peabody and Sterns in Boston but relocated to Newport where he opened an office. He became the architect of choice for wealthy Philadelphia Quakers building summer homes in Jamestown.[44] His most notable project, known as Horsehead, was built for Philadelphia industrialist Joseph Wharton.

---

[43] *Newport City Directory* 1870, 1865, https://www.*Ancestry.com*.
[44] "Jamestown Plans" *Newport Mercury* (30 June 1888), 1.

Seth Bradford

map SB

Seth Bradford (1801-1874) was born in either Rhode Island or Massachusetts, as his place of birth is noted on different US censuses. His first son Joseph was born in 1830 in Massachusetts, but his second son Augustus was born in Newport in 1837. The Newport City Directory lists his occupation as a carpenter between 1847 and 1859.

Rockry Hall- 1848
Seth Bradford architect

His existing structures are mostly in stone, and the oldest one, Rockry Hall on Bellevue Ave, was designed for Albert Sumner in the Gothic Revival style. From 1851 to 1853 he built a cottage for Mary Bruen at Howe Avenue near Bellevue, but more importantly, he completed Chateau-sur-Mer for William S. Wetmore. The structure, that featured Fall River granite, was altered between 1869 and 1880 by Richard Morris Hunt for George Peabody Wetmore. Bradford's buildings altered by later owners using other architects include Fairlawn built in 1852 for Levi Morton and Belair built in 1850 on Old Beach Road. Porter Villa,

Chateau-sur-Mer, c. 1852

built in 1856 at 23 Greenough Place, is relatively unaltered as is the 1850 Izard Cottage at 10 Pell Street. [45]

---

[45] Yarnall, 200.

James C Fludder

map JF

James Fludder 1894

James Fludder (1847-1901) was born in Newport to a stone mason from England.[46] After high school, he chose to become an architect and studied the subject in the architectural practice of George Champlin Mason.[47] After completing his work with Mason, he studied further with Henry Hobson Richardson in Boston before returning to Newport to open an office of his own at the corner of Bellevue and Catharine streets across the street from the Viking Hotel.[48] The Fludder building is now a boutique hotel called the Inn on Bellevue. In addition to a few houses in the Kay-Catherine neighborhood, he designed a number of buildings for the City of Newport including fire station #2 on Young Street (1877), the Lenthal School on Spring Street (1886), and the Townsend Industrial School (1893-94) near Newport City Hall. His last project, the Carey School, was completed in 1901 after his death at the age of 54.[49]

---

[46] Https://www.Ancestry.com.

[47] Yarnall, 67.

[48] "Death of a Well-Known Architect and Citizen," Newport Daily News (9 October 1901), http://Newspapers.com

[49] Yarnall, 202.

John Noble Alsop Griswold

map JG

J.N.A. Griswold (1822-1909) made his fortune in the China Trade between 1847 and 1854, when he was a partner in Russell and Company, the largest American company shipping goods to and from China. When Griswold returned to the United States, he invested his money in railroads and real estate in New York City.[50]

In 1860 while on his honeymoon, he and his bride met with Richard Morris Hunt and asked him to build them a house in Newport. Griswold's house, completed in 1864, was Hunt's first Newport commission.[51]

JNA Griswold House 1864
Richard Morris Hunt architect

According to Newport property records and the *Newport Mercury*, between 1860 and 1878, Griswold was involved in at least 60 instances of buying and selling property, mainly on or near Bellevue Avenue as well as along Ocean Drive.

---

[50] Application for National Landmark Status for "GRISWOLD, JOHN N.A., HOUSE." United States Department of the Interior, National Park Service, 2011, http://npgallery.nps.gov.

[51] Baker, 128.

Richard Morris Hunt

map H

Richard Morris Hunt(1827-1895) was born in Brattleboro, Vermont to a prominent family. His father, Jonathan Hunt, died while serving as a United States congressman in 1832, and in 1843 Richard's mother Jane moved the family to Europe. Richard enrolled in the Ecole des Beaux-Arts School of Architecture in 1846 and was involved with the construction of the Louvre Museum. Upon his return to the United States in 1856, he worked with Thomas Ustick Walter in the construction of the United States Capitol Building. He was a founding member of the American Institute of Architects, introduced the atelier system in America, trained other notable architects and designed a large number of significant buildings. Hunt was America's best architect.

Hunt designed about 40 buildings in Newport with the Travers Block, Marble House, Belcourt, Ochre Court and the Breakers, the most notable. He also designed the base of the statue erected in Touro Park for Matthew C. Perry.[52]

Travers Block 1871
Richard Morris Hunt architect

"Ochre Court." Residence of Mrs. Ogden Goelet, Newport, R. I.

The most complete biography of Richard Morris Hunt was written by Paul R. Baker and published in 1986.

---

[52] Baker, 538-549.

Richard Howland Hunt

map H

Richard Howland Hunt (1862-1931), son of Richard Morris Hunt, was born in Paris, graduated from Massachusetts Institute of Technology and the Ecole des Beaux-Arts. He worked with his father and served as the president of the Architecture League and the AIA in New York City.[53] Following the death of his father, he and his brother, Joseph Howland Hunt (1870-1924), continued the family firm under the name of Hunt and Hunt. The most notable project they completed was the Metropolitan Museum of Art in New York in 1902. Their Newport project was the Chinese Tea House (1912-1914) for Alva Vanderbilt Belmont on the Marble House property. The firm also added a bedroom to Belcourt for Mrs. Belmont.[54]

---

[53] "Richard H. Hunt, New York, Dies", *The Brattleboro Reformer* (14 July 1931), 1.

[54] Michael C. Kathrins, *Newport Villas* (New York: W.W. Norton and Company, Inc., 2009), 95.

Edward King

map EK

Edward King (1815-1875) was the third of four sons born to Dr. David King and Ann Gordon King in Newport. He was educated at Brown University and went on to become a partner in Russell and Sons, the largest firm in the China Trade. At that time large shippers like Russell and Company brought tea and silks which commanded high prices when sold in the United States.

King became a supervisor of cargo on a ship taking a number of trips to Canton, and each trip took many months. The work was grueling while in Canton but paid so well that the men who functioned as supervisors of cargo could retire by the age of 30 having made a fortune.[55] In a truly prophetic letter from Canton to his family in Newport, Edward King wrote:

> *"I am of the opinion that real estate in Newport will increase in value considerably in the course of a few years, and, if I were Papa, I would not sell my land except at a good price at present. Strangers will build cottages, and if factories succeed considerable addition to the population will take place. The government will no doubt in a few years have a navy yard there; perhaps not a large one at first but by degrees it will be extended...before this can come to pass, business must thrive and commerce must flourish, her wharves must be crowded with merchandise and her harbour with vessels..."[56]*

---

[55] Yarnall, 50-51.

[56] *Journal and Letters of Edward King 1835-1844.* Ed. Ethel King Russell. (New York, 1934), 82-83.

King retired in 1842 when he was just 29 and had amassed a fortune close to today's equivalent of $10 million. He hired Richard Upjohn to build his Italianate mansion on a hillside along Bowery Street with a fine view of the harbor. This was the first Italianate structure built in Newport and replaced the previously popular Gothic style country house.[57]

King invested heavily in real estate in Newport and was a business partner of Alfred Smith when Smith needed capital to expand Bellevue Avenue south.[58] Between 1844 and his death in 1875, King was involved in about 180 real estate transactions in the city of Newport, many with his fellow Newporter, JNA Griswold.

King died at the age of 60 in 1875 leaving his family well-provided for. The house remained in the family until 1912 when the family gifted the mansion to the city. It was used as the Newport Library until 1968 when it became the city's senior center.

---

[57] Yarnall, 50.
[58] Stensrud, 315-316.

Frederick Rhinelander King

map EK

The grandson of Edward King, Frederick R. King (1887-1972), was born in Newport at his parents' home at Bellevue and Berkeley Avenues. He attended St. Georges School and then Harvard, Columbia University School of Architecture and the Ecole des Beaux-Arts in Paris. He interned with McKim, Meade and White until 1918 when he joined the war effort and worked for U.S. Army Intelligence. When he returned to the United States, he interned with Carrere and Hastings before going out on his own.[59] Most of his early commissions were for family members, but in 1928, Edith Wetmore hired him to design a garden house for her at Chateau-sur-Mer. The following year she hired him to design the Seaman's Church Institute in memory of her parents. King's final Newport commission was Honyman Hall in 1955 for Trinity Church. King also designed Sea Cliff at 562 Bellevue Avenue,[60] which was purchased most recently by Larry Ellison for $11 million.

Seamen Church Institute 1930
Fredrick Rhinelander King, architect

---

[59] "Frederick King, 84, Architect, Is Dead," *New York Times*, (22 March 1972), 50.
[60] Yarnell, 206.

John G. Ladd

map JL

The earliest known project for Ladd (1807-1890) was the Greek Revival-designed structure for Captain Littlefield on Pelham Street in 1836. With its Egyptian-themed columns, it has a striking presence on the street even to this day and is best known as the home of Rhode Island Governor Charles Van Zandt. Ladd also is credited with designing 12 Catherine Street.[61] The 1850 Federal Census described Ladd as a carpenter, but in 1860 he was identified as an architect. City directories list Ladd as an architect starting in the 1850s and later directories indicate his home, Ladd Villa, on Bath Road (currently Memorial Blvd.) near Middleton Avenue. His obituary states he designed or built the best of the older summer cottages.[62]

George Champlin Mason

map GM

George C. Mason (1820-1894) was born and raised in Newport. By 1835 he was selling dry goods in New York City,[63] but in 1844 he left for Europe to improve his health.[64] While in Rome, Florence, and Paris, Mason trained as an artist. Throughout the 1850's Mason is listed in the Federal Census, Rhode Island Census and the Newport City Directories in different occupations: landscape

---

[61] Kay Street-Catherine Street-Old Beach Road Historic District National Register of Historic Places Registration Form.Https://preservation.ri.gov/sites/g/files/xkgbur406/files/pdfs_zips_downloads/national_pdfs/newport/newp_kay-catherine-old-beach-rd-hd_text.pdf.

[62] "Death of John G Ladd" *Newport Mercury* (15 November 1890), 1.

[63] "George Champlin Mason," *Biographies of Notable Americans, 1904*, https://www.Ancestry.com.

[64] US passport issued, https://www.Ancestry.com.

painter, portrait painter, drawing teacher and editor and publisher of the *Newport Mercury.*

The first mention of his career as an architect is 1858,[65] but the 1860 Federal Census lists him as a real estate agent. His first architectural project, By-the-Sea for August Belmont, dates to 1860 as well as

Chepstow, Starboard House, Gravel Court, and Narragansett Hall (all on Narragansett Avenue). These projects confirm 1860 as the start of his career as an architect. While the Belmont structure no longer exists, the ones along Narragansett Avenue provide wonderful examples of Mason's designs. His structures are often large Italianate boxes with mansard roof lines. By the end of his life, Mason was credited with designing more than 60 buildings,[66] many with his son. George Champlin Mason, Jr. joined his father as an architect in 1867 and the firm was renamed George Champlin Mason

and Son in 1871.

His best-known buildings that stand today include those on Narragansett Avenue as well as the Eisenhower House at Fort Adams and his home on Sunnyside Place. The last project completed was the 1886 chapel in Island Cemetery for the Belmont family. In addition to designing buildings, Mason trained younger aspiring architects in his

---

[65] "George Champlin Mason, *"Biographies of Notable Americans, 1904, https://www.Ancestry.com.*

[66] Yarnall, 208-209.

office, the most notable being his son, George Champlin Mason Jr., and Dudley Newton.

Mason's contributions to Newport were larger than the buildings he designed. In addition to serving as editor of the *Newport Mercury* (1851-1858) he was also a founding member of the Newport Historical Society in 1854, a trustee of the Newport Hospital beginning in 1873, a director of the Redwood Library for 30 years,[67] and an involved member of Trinity Church. He published *Newport and Its Environs* (1848), which featured 11 engravings of his landscape views of Newport. This is considered one of the earliest books about Newport to showcase its potential as a vacation destination. Mason also published *The Annals of Trinity Church: Newport, Rhode Island, 1698-1821* (1890), *Newport Illustrated* (1891) and was working on a history of the Newport Artillery Company when he died in 1894.

Alexander McGregor

map AM

Artillery Company, 1835
Alexander McGregor

One of the earliest builders of 19th century structures in Newport was Alexander McGregor (1796-1870), a stone mason by trade. He was born in Scotland in 1796 and immigrated to the United States about 1825. In 1826, he married Newporter Mary Gray.[68] His first job was overseeing the construction of Fort Adams. He went on to build what we know now as Perry Mill (1831) at the intersection of Thames, America's Cup Avenue and Memorial Boulevard. A few years after that McGregor built the Armory of the Newport Artillery Company on Clarke Street. He also erected stone walls throughout Newport and built the first breakwater on the north end of Goat Island.[69]

---

[67] "George Champlin Mason," *Appleton's Cyclopedia of American Biography, 1600-1889,* https://www.Ancestry.com.

[68] Yarnall, 291.

[69] Onorato, *AIA Guide to Newport,* 291.

In the 1840's and beyond, he turned his attention to constructing homes in the predominant style of the time, Italianate. His first residence of record was Stone Villa (1845). McGregor lived in the house with his family until 1850, when he sold it to Henry Middleton of Charleston, South Carolina. It was subsequently owned by, among others, James Gordon Bennett, publisher of the *New York Herald*, and later New York politician, William F. Whitehouse. In 1957 Whitehouse heirs sold it to a developer, who tore it down and erected the Bellevue Gardens Shopping Center.[70]

Prior to leaving Stone Villa, McGregor built a house for himself at the corner of Thomas and John Streets in 1850.[71] The following year McGregor built Swanhurst at 441 Bellevue Avenue for Judge Swan of Ohio.[72] Then he built Lansmere on Webster Street for the Eliots of Boston, and later Stoneleigh at Narragansett and Spring Streets.[73] All of those houses still exist in their original locations.

Swanhurst, 1852
Alexander McGregor

---

[70] Paul Miller, *Lost Newport* (Bedford, Massachusetts: Applewood Books, 2008), 49.

[71] Onorato, *AIA Guide to Newport*, 138.

[72] Miller, 54-55.

[73] James F. O'Gorman, *Accomplished in All Departments of Art—Hammat Billings of Boston 1818-1874* (Boston, Massachusetts: University of Massachusetts Press, 1998), 113.

Dudley Newton

map DN

Dr. Newton office 1870

Dudley Newton office 1872

Dudley Newton (1845-1907) was born in Newport to a doctor who purchased the Francis Malbone house on Thames Street in 1844. Newton grew up in Newport and trained to be an architect under George Champlin Mason.

His first known project (1865) was a church at the corner of Thames Street and Brewer Street, near the Newton home. In 1870, Newton created an office for his father that stands south of the Malbone house on Thames Street.

His practice flourished in the 1870s, and projects included his office at 20 Bellevue Avenue. Many of his residential designs exhibit stick style elements with mansard roof lines. The King-Birckhead house at 20 Catherine Street is an excellent example of this design.

Newton's projects indicate he was talented in a number of architectural styles. The 1882 the William Weld house on Bellevue Avenue exhibits Dutch or Flemish elements, and Wakehurst (1888), now part of the Salve Regina campus, is a wonderful English architectural style structure. Newton also undertook commercial projects. One of note was the Kinsley Building on Thames Street built in the Romanesque Revival style. Newton's son,

Dudley Newton Jr., joined his father in the architectural firm in Newport, but the family left the city after the death of Newton in 1907.[74]

King-Birkhead House 1872
Dudley Newton architect

Kinsley Building 1891-1893
Dudley Newton, architect

---

[74] "Dudley Newton, Jr., 67 Dies in Sacramento," *Newport Mercury* (30 April 1948), 3.

Job Almy Peckham

map JP

Peckham (1807-1885) owned a lumber yard in the city and built Italianate style homes. Some of his work stands today on Kay Street-houses at #28, #30, and #33 (his home). [75]

Alfred Smith

map AS

Alfred Smith (1809-1886) was born in Middletown, Rhode Island.[76] He trained to tailor men's clothing in Newport with Isaac Gould[77] and moved to New York City to earn his living. One of his wealthy New York clients was interested in purchasing a property in Newport and asked Smith to make the purchase when he next visited his family. Realizing that real estate might be a more lucrative occupation than tailoring, Smith left New York and returned to Newport in 1839[78] to start his new career. Six years later he developed the Kay-Catherine Street neighborhood. Smith had the vision to divide the land into building lots and create attractively landscaped streets and avenues to encourage potential customers. In 1852 he teamed with Joseph Bailey and purchased 140 acres of land south of Dixon's Lane to Bailey's Beach. Newport City Council approved the construction of a fine road connecting the site to the Kay-Catherine neighborhood, and

Smith home on Vernon Street

---

[75] Yarnall, 58.

[76] "Death of a Millionaire: Alfred Smith, Newport's Big Real Estate Agent, Dies Suddenly." *New York Times* (27 October 1886), 8.

[77] Ibid.

[78] Yarnell, 49.

Bellevue Avenue, as we know it today, was born. Smith was also a major force in building Ocean Drive to connect Bellevue Avenue to the downtown area. By the end of his life, Smith was an extremely wealthy man who handled real estate transactions, mortgages, and rentals.

Jeffrey Ladd Staats

map JS

What's unique about this gravesite is that as of 2023, Staats is still alive (1947-). He is notable because of his architectural contributions to Newport and the fact that his gravestone exists and identifies him as an architect. His projects include "Three Little Sisters", three boathouse-looking structures on Wellington Avenue across from King Park (1985c), and Wellington Square, a mixed-use development located at the intersection of Thames Street and Wellington Avenue. The Mary Street bathroom, restoration work at Cardines Field and the restoration of the Chinese Tea House at Marble House are some of his other projects.[79]

---

[79] "Jeffrey Staats," http://jeffreystaatsarchitect.com

Whitney Warren

map WW

Whitney Warren (1864-1943) was born in New York City, educated as an architect at the Ecole des Beaux- Arts in Paris, and worked mainly in New York. His projects included hotels and Grand Central Station. As a cousin to the Goelets and Vanderbilts, he had a connection to Newport and in 1894 designed the Newport Country Club, the site of the first US Open in 1895.[80]

William F Wilbor

map WFW

Wilbor(1836-1904) was a carpenter and builder in Newport. For many years he was associated with Phillip Simmons and later Frank Manchester. Houses at 7 and 9 Rhode Island Avenue were two of his projects as well as the Calvert-Cranston school. He served as a city councilman for eight years.

---

[80] "Whitney Warren, Architect, 78, Dies," *New York Times* (25 January 1943),13.

Edwin Wilbur
map EW

Born and raised in Newport, Wilbur (1867-1943) went on to study architecture at MIT and then began his practice in Newport. He designed and supervised the building of the Newport Guard Armory Building on Thames Street,[81] Engine Co. #5 on Touro Street,[82] and the receiving vault at Island Cemetery.[83] He spent the rest and the majority of his career in New York City and died at the age of 76 in Englewood Cliffs, New Jersey. He was brought back to Newport for burial.

---

[81] "Edwin Wilbur Died in Englewood, N.J.," *Newport Daily News* (29 March 1943), 7.

[82] "The City of Newport Proposal for New Engine Company," *Newport Mercury* (9 March 1895), 4.

[83] Common Burying Ground- Island Cemetery Register for Historic Places application. https://preservation.ri.gov/sites/g/files/xkgbur406/files/pdfs_zips_downloads/national_pdfs/newport/newp_farewell-street_common-burying-ground-and-island-cemetery.pdf.

chapter three

Newportant Tour

J ust about every person in this book was important to Newport, which made the decision about whom to include in this chapter challenging. The people selected made significant contributions that enhanced the city. While some were born wealthy, many earned their fortunes. Some represent 20th century middle class Americans and were businessmen or religious and civic leaders.

There are people included in other chapters of this book who were important to the city and should be included here. Since they appear elsewhere, please check their information:

Gladys Carr Bolhouse- Women's tour
Richard Morris Hunt- Architects tour
George C. Mason- Architects tour
Dudley Newton- Architects tour
Alfred Smith- Architects tour

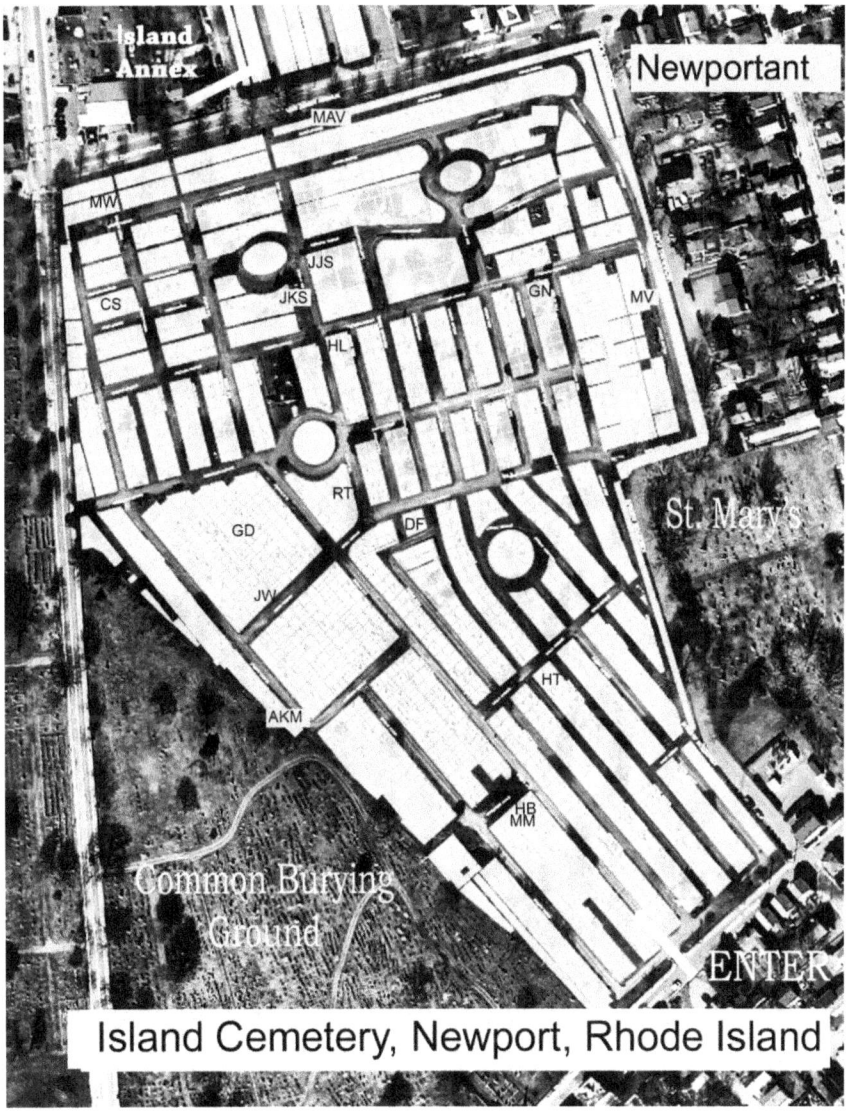

Island Cemetery, Newport, Rhode Island

Henry Bull

map HB

Henry Bull (1815-1899) was born at the family home on Bull Street. He was the sixth direct descendant from the first Henry Bull, one of the original founders of Newport. His father, Henry Bull, represented Newport in the state legislature for nearly 20 years. In 1834 with his education completed, Bull entered the counting house of his father. In 1836 Bull started a business with William Weeden and later (1843) partnered with Job Peckham. Bull was the proprietor of Bellevue House and one of the originators of the Ocean House, a hotel no longer extant. In 1870 he purchased the Buliod-Perry House and the Opera House on Washington Square and also owned Dudley Place at One Mile Corner. He was an enthusiastic farmer and served as president of the Newport Gas Light Company and Island Cemetery.[84]

Bull family house that stood near city hall

---

[84] Henry Bull Dies at Newport," *The New York Times"* (7 May 1899), 2.

George T. Downing

map GD

Downing (1819-1903) was born in New York City. His father, Thomas Downing, ran a successful restaurant that was connected to the New York Stock Exchange.[85] George Downing's limited formal education was supplemented by reading, and he became a noted speaker. He was an agent of the Underground Railway and very active  in anti-slavery societies. His first business venture in Newport, the Sea Girt Hotel, burned down in 1860, and he then built the Downing Block on Bellevue Avenue. He was one of a number of people who donated funds to the City of Newport to purchase what is now known as Touro Park, home to the Newport Tower. While his restaurant career may have started in Newport, Rhode Island, his later years spent in charge of food services at the House of Representatives in Washington, D.C., placed Downing in a perfect position to lobby lawmakers on behalf of the rights of minority populations of the country. The *Boston Evening Transcript* claimed, "His actions directly led to the opening of the Senate gallery to Negroes and to increased rights on the Baltimore and Ohio Railroad."[86] He was one of the first people to welcome to this country Louis Kossuth (fighter for Hungary's freedom from Austria), was a friend of labor, and sided with foreign- born people fighting for equal rights in Rhode Island. When he died in 1903, the *Boston Globe* stated that Downing was probably "the foremost colored man in the country."[87]

---

[85] Leader of Colored Race," *The Fall River Daily Herald (31 December 1902)*, 1.

[86] "George T Downing," *Boston Evening Transcript* (22 July 1903), 11.

[87] "George T. Downing, "*The Boston Globe* (23 July 1903), 6.

Daniel Fearing

map DF

Fearing (1859-1918) was born in Newport and during the summer season lived in his parents' house near the ocean. "The Cliffs" was believed to have been designed and built by George Champlin Mason prior to 1860.[88] Fearing inherited the house when his father died in 1886.

Fearing's obituary emphasized his involvement in civic betterment in Newport. He served on the school committee, the Board of Aldermen and as mayor for a term. He was also a member of the State Board of Commissioners of Island Fisheries for the protection of fish. He served as president of both the Newport Historical Society and the Redwood Library.

He was an integral part of the Newport Chapter of the Red Cross and was in the process of giving final instructions for a concert on the beach to benefit the group when he collapsed and died.[89]

---

[88] Miller, 35.

[89] "Daniel B. Fearing," *Newport Mercury* (31 May 1918), 4.

Henry Ledyard

map HL

Henry Ledyard (1812-1880) was born in New York City, attended Columbia college, and practiced law in New York. In 1836 he became personal assistant to Lewis Cass, who had been named Minister to France by Andrew Jackson. Ledyard married Cass's daughter in 1839.

When Cass returned to the United States in 1844, Ledyard settled in Michigan, where Cass had been territorial governor. Ledyard went on to serve both Cass and the City of Detroit, even spending a year as mayor of that city.

Ledyard was elected to the U.S. Senate in 1857 but resigned his seat when Cass was named Secretary of State. Ledyard accompanied Cass to Washington and remained there until 1861.

During the Civil War, Ledyard moved to Newport and had a house built at the corner of Catherine and Ayrault Streets, which is now a condominium building called Cloverleigh. The house was designed and built by George Champlain Mason.[90]

Ledyard became heavily involved in helping to found Newport Hospital. He led the fundraising for the original 12 bed facility because he felt that the trip to the hospital in Providence was too long, especially in winter, and would increase suffering and decrease the chances of recovery. He served as the first president of the hospital from 1873-1879.[91] Ledyard also served as president of the Redwood Library.

In 1880 while on a trip to London, Henry Ledyard died. His body was brought back for burial in Island Cemetery.

---

[90] Silas Farmer, *The History of Detroit and Michigan* (Detroit, Michigan: S. Farmer and Company, 1889), 104-1043.

[91] "History of Newport Hospital," http://lifespan.org/locations/newport-hospital

The false sarcophagus for the family plot was designed by Richard Morris Hunt.[92]

Mark Malkovich III

map MM

Mark Malkovich (1930-2010) was born in Minnesota. As a child he played the clarinet and learned to play piano at age 15. During the Korean War, he served in the Minnesota National Guard and later attended Columbia University, graduating with a degree in chemistry in 1954. He also took private lessons on piano with a teacher from Juilliard. In 1959 he married Joan Shewring, and they spent several years in Belgium, where he worked for a chemical company.

When the Malkovichs returned to the United States, they bought a house in Newport, and Malkovich was asked by the board of the Newport Music Festival if he would take on the position of director. He agreed to a one-year trial period but insisted he not be paid. He ran the festival for 35 years emphasizing, in his words, "Rare, rather than common fare."

In late May 2010, Malkovich died in a car accident while in Minnesota. Later that year on his 80th birthday, what had been planned as a birthday celebration concert at the Breakers mansion turned into a memorial for the late director.[93]

---

[92] Farmer, 1041.

[93] Bryan Marquard, "Mark Malkovich; Brought New Music Talent to Newport," *Boston Globe* (4 June 2010). Archive. boston.com/bostonglobe/obituaries.

Andrew Kirk McMahon

map AKM

McMahon (1841-1921) was born in Ireland, and his family immigrated to America in 1846. When he was old enough, McMahon became a day laborer like his father while living in the Providence area.

Andrew Kirk McMahon
1841-1921

After serving in the army during the Civil War, Andrew McMahon relocated to Newport in 1871 to take the position of head gardener on the Robert H. Ives estate just off Cliff Walk. After Ives' death the estate was sold, and McMahon was elected Superintendent of Island Cemetery. He continued in that position until his death in 1921.

He was extremely active in organizations in Newport including, among many others, the Masonic Lodge and the Oddfellows. He also served as Commander of the Charles E. Lawton Post of the G.A.R. In addition, he was a junior warden at Emmanuel Church for 35 years.[94]

---

[94] "Andrew K. McMahon," *Newport Mercury* (6 August 1921), 1.

George H. Norman

map GN

George Norman (1827-1900) was born in Newport, had a public-school education, and started work at age 14 as a clerk in a store. He later opened a shoe store at Thames Street and Market Square. In 1846 Norman was involved in establishing the *Newport Daily News* with William H. Cranston. Norman became the first secretary of the company that introduced natural gas to the city, and with his acquired knowledge, installed gas works at Santiago, Chile and West Point, New York. The installation of waterworks was more to his liking, and he did so throughout New England and the United States. In 1878 Norman established the Newport Waterworks.[95] Building and installing waterworks made George Norman a very wealthy man. Pictured below is his home, Belaire, located on Old Beach Road near Red Cross Avenue.

---

[95] "George H. Norman," *Newport Mercury* (10 February 1900), 1.

John Jermain Slocum, Jr

map JJS

Jerry Slocum (1941-2017), as he was known, was born in New York City. He was descended from Myles Standish on his father's side of the family and from Roger Williams on his mother's side. Mr. Slocum received both his M.A. and M.B.A from Harvard and entered the field of investment banking. He began his career working for S.C. Warburg and then Brown Brothers Harriman. He ran for the United States Congress in both 1976 and 1978, and later in 1978 he formed the firm of Slocum, Gordon & Company.

Slocum always had a great interest in genealogy and developed an interest in history. He was the long-time director of the Alletta Morris McBean Charitable Trust, a director of the Redwood Library, and the president and CEO of the Preservation Society of Newport County from 1989-1999.

He served as a president of the Harvard Business School Association of Southeastern New England, as president of the Society of the Cincinnati of Rhode Island, and as chairman of the Library Committee of the Society of the Cincinnati in Washington, D.C.[96]

---

[96] "Deaths," *New York Times* (20 August 2017), 21.

Clarence Stanhope

map CS

Stanhope photograph of Beacon Rock

Clarence Stanhope (1852-1924) was born in Newport and later employed as a clerk and bookkeeper in local businesses. In 1882 he was hired as cashier and bookkeeper at the Newport Casino, a job he continued in until shortly before his death.[97] While his time at the Casino contributed to the success of this important Newport institution, Stanhope is important to the city for his work as an amateur photographer. The *Newport Mercury* reported that he has taken a number of photographs of buildings in the city.[98] In 1891 he published a guidebook to Newport, "In and Around Newport."[99] His photographs are part of many museum collections including the Newport Historical Society, the Newport Public Library, the Getty Museum and the Library of Congress. These images are invaluable in documenting the history of the city.

---

[97] "Clarence Stanhope," *Newport Mercury* (8 November 1924), 1.

[98] "Mr. Clarence Stanhope," *Newport Mercury* (27 August 1887), 1.

[99] Federico Santi, "Who is Clarence Stanhope?" *Newport This Week Now* (22 October, 2020), https://www.newportthisweek.com/articles/who-was-clarence-stanhope.

Jeremiah Kirrian Sullivan

map JKS

Jeremiah Sullivan (1857-1939), born in Newport, was a general contractor, street commissioner, banker, and director of several corporations. During his service as streets commissioner, granite block paving was installed on Thames Street which bear his initials to this day at the Green Street intersection. Known widely as JK, he was well-known in the city and to the summer residents with whom he was engaged in business (mainly through the New York Yacht Club). Starting as a carpenter's apprentice, he went into the express business and later operated a large livery stable business that included 75-90 horses and over 100 wagons. He later conducted a general contracting business and worked on a number of large projects in Newport, including Rough Point. Sullivan added boat work to this portfolio of businesses with links to the New York Yacht Club and Arthur Curtiss James. He constructed a building on Bellevue Avenue adjacent to the Newport Reading Room. Sullivan served as a trustee of the Newport Trust Company and director of the Newport Gas Light Company. He donated a marble altar to St. Mary's Church and in 1913 advanced money to Newport teachers when city funds were so low that teachers would not have been paid. [100]

J.K. SULLIVAN

Entance floor

Arch above entrance

---

[100] "Jeremiah K. Sullivan Dies Wednesday," *Newport Mercury* (10 March 1939), 1.

Dr. Roderick Terry

map RT

Roderick Terry (1849-1933) was born in Brooklyn, New York in 1849. He went on to attend Yale and later Princeton and was ordained into the Presbyterian ministry in 1875. He served as minister for 27 years at two different churches as well as chaplain of a regiment of the New York State National Guard from 1890-1900.

After 24 years as pastor of the South Reformed Church in New York City, he and his wife, Linda Marquand Terry, came to live in Newport. Terry immediately became involved in a number of organizations in Newport, serving as president of both the Newport Historical Society and the Redwood Library from 1918 until 1930. He purchased several Revolutionary War forts in Newport County on behalf of the Newport Historical Society as well as spearheading the installation of and payment for the statue of Rochambeau in King Park in the summer of 1928. In addition, Terry played a part in the restoration of the Colony House and the expansion of the Redwood Library.[101]

---

[101] "Dr. Roderick Terry Died This Afternoon," *Newport Mercury and Weekly News* (29 December 1933), 2.

Dr. Henry E. Turner

map HT

Henry Turner (1816-1897) was born in Warwick, Rhode Island to a family with direct ties to men who started the colony and fought in the American Revolution. He was educated in East Greenwich and after the family moved to Portsmouth, he studied medicine with his uncle and father, Drs. William and James V. Turner. After graduating in 1836 with a medical degree from the University of Pennsylvania, Turner joined his father in his Newport practice. He tended the people of Newport for 60 years and took an interest in public affairs.

He served as a member of the school committee for 19 years, a director of the Redwood Library for 39 years, a member of the Rhode Island Medical Society, president of the Newport Medical Society and additional medical organizations. Turner served in the United States Army at Fort Adams from 1862 to 1865. His practice in Newport was shared with three generations of doctors that included both Dr. David Kings.[102]

Turner was also a member and president of the Newport Historical Society and wrote extensively about Rhode Island's early history. He served as secretary of the Willow Cemetery for a number of years. He wrote an article for the historical society "Monumental Inscriptions, Newport R.I." in 1881 that helped document burials in the city.[103] His work was one of the four major transcripts of gravestones in the Common Burying Ground.

---

[102] "Full of Years and Honors, Long and Useful Career of Dr. Henry E. Turner Closed," *Newport Daily News* (3 June 1897), 6.

[103] John Sterling et al., *Newport, Rhode Island Colonial Burial Grounds* (Hope, Rhode Island: Rhode Island Genealogical Society, 2009), xxiii.

Mahlon van Horne

map MV

Reverend Mahlon Van Horne (1840-1910) was born in Princeton, New Jersey and educated at Lincoln University. In 1869 after teaching in New York and South Carolina, he accepted a position to pastor the

congregation in Newport, Rhode Island at the Union Congregational Church. During his 28 years of leading the congregation, the group moved to Division Street and membership swelled to 223 members. With the help of George Downing, Van Horne became the first person of color to be elected to the Newport School Committee (1872), a position he held for 20 years. He was also the first person of color to be elected to the Rhode Island Legislature (1885) and served three terms. In 1897 President McKinley appointed Van Horne as consul to St. Thomas, a post he held until 1903. Van Horne advocated the purchase of the Danish West Indies by the United States, an action that took place in 1917, making them the U.S. Virgin Islands. [104]

---

[104] Patrick T. Conley, "My Turn- Rhode Island's First Black Legislator," *Providence Journal* (9 February 2021), A11.

John Goddard Weaver

map JW

John Weaver (1812-1892) was born in Newport, educated locally and joined his father and brother Joseph (1810-1873) in the hat making business. He and Joseph later started a stable business and oversaw the horses of the Newport Artillery Company. In 1842, John Weaver was involved in the events at Federal Hill in Providence against Thomas Dorr and his followers. He later represented Newport in the State Assembly in 1841-1842 and in 1854-1876 was a member of Newport City Council. His major impact on Newport was the construction and operation of the Ocean House Hotel at Bellevue Avenue and Berkeley Street (currently the Stop and Shop Center). The hotel opened in 1844 as a four-story, 122 room place to accommodate the growing numbers of summer travelers. It burned to the ground a year later, and Weaver rebuilt a 600-bed hotel that was ready to serve the summer guests in 1846. [105] Joseph Weaver, John's brother, owned and operated the Atlantic House at the corner of Pelham Street and Bellevue Avenue (built 1845) with John's financial backing.[106] The Atlantic House served as the location of the Naval Academy during the Civil War but was not owned at that time by Joseph Weaver, who had sold the hotel in 1858. The hotels and John Weaver were the beginning of Newport's rebirth.

Ocean House on Bellevue Avenue

---

[105] "Death of John G Weaver," *Newport Mercury*, (13 August 1892), 1.
[106] Stensrud, 304.

Matthias Alonzo Van Horne

map MAV

Matthias Van Horne (1871-1932) was born in Newport to Mahlon Van Horne, a prominent minister, Newport school commissioner, state representative, and U.S. Consul. The younger Van Horne attended Newport public schools and commercial college where he studied dentistry. He was the first African American dentist in the state when he opened his practice at the family home at 47 John Street in 1896. In addition to his dental practice, Dr. Van Horne was active in the Stone Mill Lodge of the Masons as well as other fraternal organizations. An

Matthias Alonzo Van Horne
1871-1932

active member of his father's church (Union Congregational), he also served on their Board of Trustees and chaired the board for 14 years. He was one of the founding members of the Newport Chapter of the NAACP. Dr. Matthias Alonzo Van Horne collapsed while attending a lodge meeting and died a short time later at the Newport Hospital.[107]

---

[107] "Sudden Death of Dr. M.A. Van Horne," *Newport Mercury* (5 February 1932), 3.

Dr. Marcus Wheatland

map MW

Marcus Wheatland (1868-1934) was born in Barbados in 1868 and educated in private schools. In 1887 he enrolled at Howard University and obtained his medical degree. According to the Rhode Island Black Heritage Society, in 1894 Wheatland relocated to Newport because of his relationships with Matthias Van Horne and George T. Downing. He was licensed to practice medicine in Rhode Island in 1895. In 1898 Dr. Wheatland married Irene De Mortie, granddaughter of Mr. Downing, at Trinity Church in Copley Square in Boston.

Wheatland was the first doctor in Newport to use the x-ray machine as a diagnostic tool and owned the first x-ray machine in the city. He was a member of numerous medical societies including the American Medical Association and was at one time president of the National Medical Association. In addition, he served on the Newport City Council and was a trustee of Howard University. He died at the age of 66 from longstanding heart problems.[108]

---

[108] "Dr. Wheatland Dead, After Long Illness," *Newport Mercury and Weekly News* (17 August 1934), 2.

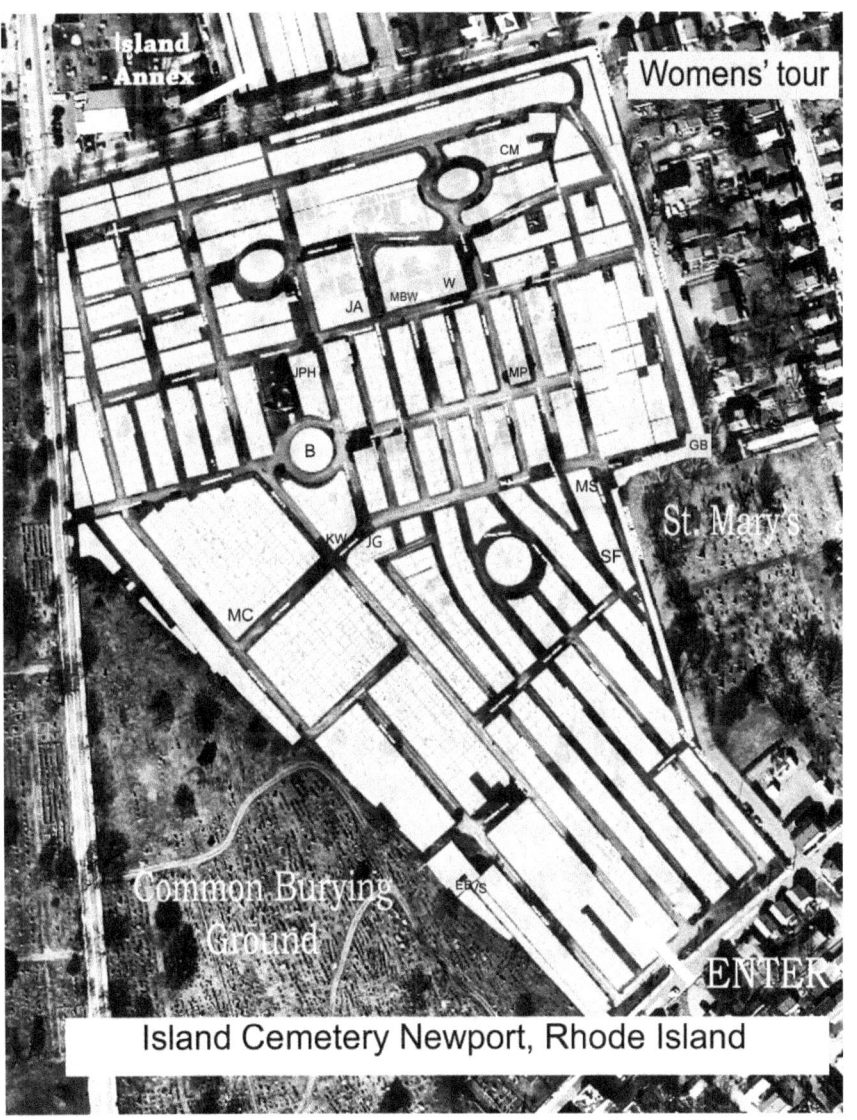

Island Annex

Womens' tour

CM

JA MBW W

JPH MP

B GB

MS

KW JG St. Mary's

SF

MC

Common Burying Ground EBS

ENTER

Island Cemetery Newport, Rhode Island

CHAPTER 4

The Women of Island Cemetery

O ne of the most frustrating situations people find when walking through an old cemetery is to see etched above a woman's name "daughter of" or "wife of" or "mother of." Regardless of a woman's economic status, she was almost always defined by her relationship to a man.

Newspaper obituaries for women were rare until well into the 20th century. Even a wealthy and well-respected woman like Ethel Rhinelander King, who should have been recognized for her contributions to the arts and society in both New York and Newport, was a footnote in her own obituary. Her multi-paragraph obituary in the *New York Times* discussed her father, her husband and the minister who conducted the funeral service. It included the fact that the chapel in which her service was conducted had been built by the King family, but no mention was ever made about her good works.

The women included in this chapter/tour are included solely for their accomplishments independent of the men in their lives. Additional research will undoubtedly find many additional women buried here who are worthy of inclusion.

Janet Auchincloss

map JA

Janet Lee Bouvier Auchincloss Morris (1907-1989) was born in New York City. Her father was a lawyer and real estate developer, and the family was Irish Catholic. She attended Barnard College but did not graduate. In 1928 she married John Bouvier III and subsequently gave birth to daughters Jacqueline and Caroline Lee. Janet Bouvier was an accomplished rider and won 3 national championships at the National Horse Show held in New York City. She divorced Bouvier in 1942 due to his heavy drinking and womanizing. Later that same year, she married Hugh Dudley Auchincloss Jr, and the couple remained married until his death in 1976. She

Janet Auchincloss holds her child. Jacqueline, her daughter, is seated at the top of the steps.

served as a board member of the Newport Historical Society and the Redwood Library. When her daughter married Senator John Kennedy, the wedding took place in Newport with a reception at her home, Hammersmith Farm.[109]

---

[109] "Janet Lee Auchincloss," *New York Times* (24 July 1989), D11.

Eleanor Robson Belmont

map B

Eleanor Robson (1878-1979) was born in Lancashire, England, the third generation of a theatrical family. Her father died when she was young, and when her mother remarried, the family moved to the United States. She began her acting career at age 17 in San Francisco. Her career took her to New York and later London, where she was applauded by J.M. Barrie and G.B. Shaw. George Bernard Shaw was very taken with her and wrote "Major Barbara" for her. He also wrote her numerous love letters.

She was an acclaimed actress but gave up her career in 1910 to became the second wife of August Belmont Jr. She spent the rest of her life working for charitable and artistic causes. She founded the

Eleanor Robson Belmont
1879-1979

Metropolitan Opera Guild in 1935 to raise money for the company and served as the first woman elected to the board of directors of the company in 1933. Eleanor Belmont was also a crusader for the Red Cross and made several trips to Europe during World War I. In 1917 she carried a letter to General Pershing from President Roosevelt. She died at age 99 in her sleep at her home in New York.[110]

---

[110] "Eleanor R. Belmont Dies at 100; Leader in Charities and the Arts," *New York Times*, (25 October 1979), 1.

Gladys Carr Bolhouse

map GB

Gladys Carr (1899-1995) was born in Rhode Island and married Peter Bolhouse July 13, 1928.[111] The 1930 Federal Census shows her living with her parents and newborn son Daniel, and the 1940 Federal Census shows the addition of daughters Jane and Mary. Peter Bolhouse, a WWI Navy veteran, died in 1955, and it was after this year Gladys Bolhouse began working at the Newport Historical Society. In 1957 and 1958 she was the executive secretary of the organization, and in the 1970s she was the curator of manuscripts. In 1984 she was named the first official historian of the City of Newport. Gladys Bolhouse spoke at numerous group meetings and was frequently quoted on historical matters in the newspapers. She was an active member of St. Paul's Methodist Church and the Major William Taggart Chapter of the DAR.[112]

[111] "Married in Kay Chapel," *Newport Mercury* (13 July 1928), 8.

[112] Richard Champlin, "Tribute to Gladys Bolhouse," *Newport History*: Vol. 67: Issue 231, Article 4, https://digitalcommons.salve.edu/newporthistory/vol67/iss231/4.

Edith Bozyan

map EB

Edith Bozyan (1908-1993) was an important figure in the local art world. She was born in Newport and educated in Newport's public school system. At the age of ten, she received a scholarship to classes given by the Art Association in the Griswold House on Bellevue Avenue. She attended Smith College, graduating in 1929, and moved to New York to study at the Art Students League. There she rented stu-

Edith Bozyan 1907-1993

dio space from classmate Jackson Pollack. One of her instructors at the Art Students League was artist Thomas Hart Benton, whom she remembered years later as a "male chauvinist pig." She went on to teach art in some of New York's public schools and exhibited her work at the Art Association in Newport from 1930 on. In 1950 she returned to Newport to help her father run his antique business at 138 Bellevue Avenue, now the site of Pasta Beach Restaurant.[113]

In August 1984 artist and patron, Edith Bozyan, got fellow artists together to form a group to show contemporary art in her father's former antique shop and named it DeBlois Gallery. It was the first artists co-op on Aquidneck Island and has been continuously running since 1984 to showcase the work of local artists from Rhode Island and southeastern Massachusetts.[114] In 2014 DeBlois Gallery moved to Valley Road in Middletown, Rhode Island.

---

[113] "Edith Bozyan, "*MacDowell News* (Peterborough, NH), http://www.macdowell.org/artists/edith-bozyan.

[114] "DeBlois Gallery Celebrates 30 Years," *The Bay Magazine* (29 May 2014).

Marion Kalsholhen Carry

map MC

Carry (1905-1987) was born at 12 Friendship Street in Newport and lived there her entire life. In 1926 she graduated from the Rhode Island School of Design and later began a career that ran for five decades of teaching art at the Newport Art Association. At first, she assisted Helena Sturtevant and was noted in the writings of Association founder Maud Howe Elliott. In 1938 Carry was awarded a scholarship by the Association that allowed her to study art in Europe.[115]

State cemetery records indicate Marion was cremated at Swan Point Cemetery in Providence. Island Cemetery records indicate that Marion's remains are buried here, but she is not included on the family monument.

---

[115] "Exhibit Remembers A Newport Original," *Newport Daily News* (14 June 2013), http://newportri.com

Susan Braley Franklin

map SF

Susan B. Franklin (1868-1955) was born in Newport in 1868 to a family that had a bakery in the city. She attended Bryn Mawr College,

achieving her B.A. in 1889 and her PhD in 1896. She paid for graduate school by teaching Latin at Vassar.

Franklin taught first at Miss Baldwin's School near Bryn Mawr College but then headed the classical department at the Workingman's School from 1904-1933. When her aging parents needed help, she returned to Newport and finished out her teaching career at Rogers High School.

Franklin was a member of the Society for Cultural Studies and was the first woman to have an article published in their scholastic journal. She was extremely interested in history and contributed a great deal of research to the Newport Historical Society.

Sadly, Miss Franklin was murdered in her home when she was 86 years old. In her will, she left all her money to establish scholarships for students at Brown and Bryn Mawr.[116]

---

[116] John O.C. McCrillis, "Thanks to Susan Braley Franklin, Scholar and Mentor," *Newport History:* Vol. 64: Iss. 221, Article 5 (1991). https://digitalcommons.salve.edu/newporthistory/vol64/iss221/5

Ward Briggs, "Franklin, Susan Braley," Database of Classical Scholars, Rutgers School of Arts and Sciences, https://dbcs.rutgers.edu/all-scholars/9324-franklin-susan-braley.

Jane Emmet Griswold

map JG

Jane Emmet (1832-1909) was born in Charlottesville, Virginia in 1832 and spent the first ten years of her life there. After her father's death, Jane and her mother relocated to New York City and lived with Jane's older brother, an eminent obstetrician/gynecologist.[117]

Jane Emmet married the wealthy John Noble Alsop Griswold in 1860, and they honeymooned throughout Europe for about two years. She kept a series of journals and showed a proclivity for writing.

In addition to giving birth to five children and running the household, she pursued her own interests. In 1870 the official publication of the National Woman Suffrage Association praised Jane Griswold for her kindness in inviting the children from the Orphans Home of Newport into her home. She also invited Julia Ward Howe to use her home for meetings of the Town and Country Club, an organization of both male and female intellectuals.

Sometime around 1890, Jane Griswold left her husband and home in Newport. In August of 1892, JNA Griswold added a codicil to his will which changed his bequest to his wife:

> *"Whereas my wife Jane Emmet has seen fit without just cause from me to accept an annuity of $6000 per annum (just over $1 million today) and*

---

[117] J. Doyle, "Jane Emmet," 29 February 2012, *emmetry,* http://emmetrydevelopment.com/people/janeemmet.

to live separate and apart from me...I direct that she receive what the law provides as her right of dower in my real estate."[118]

Jane Griswold purchased a flat in New York City and a home in the artists' colony, Onteora Park, in the Catskills. Candace Wheeler, the founder of the colony, wrote of Jane Griswold in her memoir, *Yesterdays in a Busy Life*: "Among the very first who were so caught by the glamour of the mountains as to make their homes there were Mary Mapes Dodge...Susan Coolidge...and Mrs. J.N.A. Griswold, born Emmet, with even more than her share of the Emmet brilliancy sparkling in all she did."[119]

During her time in the Catskills, Jane Griswold wrote a novel called *The Lost Wedding Ring* featuring the character of Letitia Boy. It isn't much of a stretch to call the book an autobiography. Mrs. Boy was also separated from her husband but chose not to ask for a divorce because she did not want to bring the marriage any lower by opening herself and her family members to scandal. She went on to discuss how the modern woman could no longer promise to obey her husband and was quite capable of standing on her own two feet. Mrs. Griswold, like her character Mrs. Boy, blamed her husband for putting too much importance on money, and she believed he had caused the premature deaths of two of their sons by insisting they work harder than they were able to.

The Griswold's lived apart for the rest of their lives, and Jane Griswold spent the bulk of her time in New York. She was often cited in newspaper articles as an avid reader and attendee of literary soirees. She died at her home in January 1909, and after her funeral, her body was returned to Newport for burial in the family plot near the graves of the three sons who predeceased her. Her husband died eight months later and was buried next to her.

---

[118] Last will and testament of John Noble Alsop Griswold on file at the Newport County Courthouse, Newport, Rhode Island.

[119] Candace Wheeler, *Yesterdays in a Busy Life* (New York: Harper, 1918), 268.

Jane Pickens Hoving

map JPH

Jane Pickens (1907-1992) began life in Georgia where she and her sisters formed a singing trio. They had a radio show in New York in the 1930s. Pickens was part of the Ziegfeld Follies of 1936 and appeared in some films and on Broadway.

Jane Pickens Hoving
1907-1992

In 1971 she purchased a Colonial Revival mansion on Bellevue Avenue designed by Ogden Codman in 1910. A few years later, Jane Pickens and her sister gave a concert at the former Strand Theater on Washington Square, and the owner named the theater in her honor.

Jane Pickens died at her house in Newport in 1992. Her estate was inherited by her only daughter, Marcella Clark McCormack.[120]

Princess Alexandra Troubetzkoy Malcom

map CM

Alexandra Troubetzkoy (1910-1994) was born in Russia in 1910 to an aristocratic family. Like many Russian aristocrats, the family fled Russia in 1919 after the October Revolution. *Downton Abbey* fans may recall the old flame of the Dowager Countess Grantham who ended up in London after fleeing Russia.

Alexandra Troubetzkoy was educated in England and France and began to study art at age ten. Later she trained at the Art Students League in New York and at the National Academy of Design. She also

---

[120] "Jane Pickens Hoving Dies at 83," *New York Times* (24 February 1992), B10.

attended the Ruskin School of Drawing and studied fine arts at Oxford University.

After the death of her first husband in Italy, she came to the United States and had her first exhibition in New York in 1955. There she met her second husband with whom she is buried here. Most of her art is in museums and in private collections.[121]

Marcella Clark McCormack

map JPH

Marcella Clark McCormack (1930-2010), the only child of Jane Pickens, was known as a conservationist and arborist. She set aside more than two acres of her estate, Merrillton on Bowery Street, for the Aquidneck Land Trust which is called "Marcella's Woods." A few years after her death, the A.L.T received $2.8 million from her to pur-

chase land in the future for the trust.[122]

[121] "A. Troubetzkoy, 84, Princess and Artist." *New York Times* (5 July 1994), D14.
[122] "Land Trust Receives Large Gift." *Newport This Week* (31 January 2014), 2.

Mildred Olive Bigelow Tilton Pell

map MP

Mildred Olive Bigelow (1886-1980) was an artist and author known to many as Olive Bigelow Pell. She studied art at the Art Students League in New York, and in Paris and in Munich.[123] Her work was widely exhibited in the United States and Europe. Her portrait work

was sold to raise funds for the American Red Cross during WWI, and during WWII, her work provided funds for the American and British Red Cross. [124] She wrote and illustrated "Belinda," a book about her time in Europe as the wife of a U.S. diplomat, and illustrated two history books. In 1952 she published a condensed version of the *King James Bible* that took 12 years to create. Her version of the Bible is about 20% the length of the original since her goal was to make it more readable for the average person.[125] In a 1930 when she became a grandmother, she took her own advice that every grandmother ought to have a career, so at age 43, Mrs. Pell returned to painting.[126] Her rationale for this advice was that grandmothers should not interfere with raising the grandchildren or be pests or bosses in their homes.

---

[123] AskART Archives Biography, https://www.askart.com/artist/Olive_Pell/120956/Olive_Pell.aspx

[124] "Olive Pell, 94, A Painter: Works Helped Red Cross," *New York Times* (10 December 1980), D23.

[125] Ibid.

[126] "Mrs. Pell, Urging Careers for Grandmothers, Returns, as Olive Bigelow, to Painting at 43," *New York Times* (15 January 1930), 27.

Virginia Beans Sampson

map VS

Virginia Beans Sampson (1908-2001) was born in Massachusetts and married Norman Sampson before 1930. The 1930 United States Census shows that she was a bookkeeper at the Island Cemetery. In 1997 John Sterling, who was documenting burials in Newport, visited Sampson, and she shared she had been with the cemetery for 70 years. Her affiliation with the site was the longest of any individual. In addition to her work at the cemetery, Sampson was active in the business community. In 1937 she was active in the Newport Business and Professional Women's Club and served as its president.[127] In 1938 she was elected vice-president of the Rhode Island Professional Women's Club and led the organization in 1939.[128] Sampson also served as president of the Hope Branch of the International Sunshine Foundation.[129]

Maud Lyman Stevens

map MS

Maud Stevens (1869-1949) was a respected author, historian, and authority on Newport and Rhode Island history. She served as a director of the Newport Historical Society and published the society bulletin. One of her most notable papers was the history of the Vernon House on Clarke Street. Additionally, Ms. Stevens was an avid gardener and member of the Newport and Jamestown Garden Clubs. She was an active member of Channing Church, the Newport Art Association, the Rhode Island Society of Colonial Dames, the Current Topics Club, and vice-president of the Home for the Aged-on Washington Street.[130]

---

[127] "News Briefs," *Newport Mercury and Weekly News* (30 July 1937), 7.

[128] "Newporter Heads State Women's Body: Mrs. Virginia Sampson Elected President of RI Club," *Newport Mercury and Weekly News* (9 June 1939), 5.

[129] "Hope Branch Marks 70th Anniversary," *Newport Mercury* (19 October 1973), 5.

[130] "Maud L. Stevens Dies; Writer, Historian," *Newport Mercury and Weekly News* (18 November 1949), 3.

Maud Barger Wallach

map MBW

Maud Barger Wallach (1870-1954) was inducted into the Tennis Hall of Fame in 1958. She was a right-handed baseline player with an accurate forehand but weak backhand.[131] In 1906 and 1909 she was the runner-up at the US National Championship tournament and captured the championship in 1908 from Evelyn Sears in 3 sets. Wallach was also an active fox hunter and ice skater.[132] Much to the dismay of other skaters, she rented the St. Nicholas Ice Rink in Washington, D.C. three times a week for private lessons with John Davidson, a champion fancy skater.[133]

Maud Barger Wallach
1870-1954

Wallach was a governor at the Newport Casino[134] and donated the championship trophy awarded at the Casino. In a 1940 interview she gave to a reporter from the *Brownsville Herald*, the 70-year-old Wallach told the reporter she was dissatisfied with her game and planned to change her forehand. [135] Maud Barger Wallach was chair of the committee that first ranked women tennis players in the United States.

Wallach's family were longtime summer visitors to Newport and their father bought the Isaac Bell House. Following his death, Maud

---

[131] "Maud Barger-Wallace", *Wikipedia*. https://en.wikipedia.org/wiki/Maud_Barger-Wallach

[132] "Mrs. Barger Wallach Dies, '08 National Tennis Champ," *Newport Daily News* (2 April 1954), 2.

[133] "Hires Rink to Skate Alone," *The Washington Post* (21 December 1914), 6.

[134] "Edna H. Barger, Summer Colonist," *Newport Daily News* (20 May 1957) ,2.

[135] "Proving It's Never Too Late," *Brownsville Herald* (9 August 1940), 7.

and her sister, Edna Barger (1872-1957), continued to live in the Isaac Bell House on Bellevue Avenue. The house was in the Barger family longer than any other owner of the property (1891-1952).[136] After the family sold the property, it became a nursing home and was eventually acquired by the Preservation Society of Newport County. If you visit the property, you may notice on the Perry Street entrance the name "Edna Villa" carved into the gate post. The house was named for the mother of Edna and Maud, Mrs. Edna Barger.

Isaac Bell House

---

[136] Isaac Bell, Jr House, National Historic Landmark Nomination, https://npgallery.nps.gov/GetAsset/c42ec182-1cba-4454-883c-9f07ba7666bb, 11.

Edith Wetmore and Maud Wetmore

map W

Edith
Wetmore

Maud Wetmore

The Wetmore sisters were two of the most well-known women in Newport and New York. Since neither had to look for a husband or a job, both remained single, a phenomenon somewhat common to women of their class.

Edith Wetmore was born in 1870 in Switzerland while her parents were on their extended honeymoon. Maud Wetmore was born in Paris three years later. The sisters spent the bulk of their lives at the family home, Chateau-sur-Mer, or at their New York townhouse at 1 Beekman Place.

They commissioned and paid for the Seamen's Church Institute in Newport as a memorial to their parents as well as donating to numerous charities. Both women were original members of the Preservation Society of Newport County, and the first meeting of the group took place at Chateau-sur-Mer, with Maud Wetmore elected as the first president.

Apart from that, their individual interests and activities varied greatly. Edith Wetmore was an integral part of the Cooper-Hewitt Museum in New York, and she and her sister donated many family heirlooms to the collections there. She also donated a collection of first editions and rare children's books to the Providence Library. She was a charter member and great financial supporter of the Newport Art Association when they formed in 1912 and loaned family paintings to the group for exhibitions. She was also the long-time president of the Old Statehouse Committee to maintain the integrity of what is now known as the Colony House.

While her sister was involved mostly in New York City, Newport and Rhode Island groups, Maud Wetmore was busy with more national affairs. She was involved in Republican Party politics, especially in New York, and also a leader in the Committee on Women's Defense Work during World War I. Oddly, neither she nor her sister ever supported women's suffrage.

Maud Wetmore was an avid player of both golf and tennis, reaching the finals of the U.S. Women's Amateur Golf Tournament in 1898. She also loved to drive her own car.

Maud Wetmore died unexpectedly in 1951 at her Newport home while Edith lived until 1966 to the age of 95. Chateau-sur-Mer was willed to the Society for the Preservation of New England Antiquities, but the group declined. In 1969 the Preservation Society of Newport County purchased the home from Edith Wetmore's estate.[137]

---

[137] "Maude Wetmore Dead in Newport," *New York Times* (4 November 1951), 85; "Edith Wetmore of Newport Dies," *New York Times* (11 March 1966), 25.

Katherine Prescott Wormeley

map KW

Kathrine Prescott Wormeley (1830-1908) was born in England to a British-American couple. She emigrated to America in 1848 and dur-

ing the American Civil War nursed Union soldiers. Her work as a volunteer for the U.S. Sanitary Commission included serving as a matron on a hospital ship and as superintendent of Lowell General Hospital in Portsmouth Grove, Rhode Island. She founded the Newport Charity Organization Society in 1874 and established an industrial school to educate working class girls in 1887.[138]

She was also an excellent translator of French literature and is known in literary circles for translations of Moliere, Balzac, Dumas and other French authors. Her home on Red Cross Avenue was designed by McKim, Mead, and White.

---

[138] "Katherine Wormeley," Library of Congress- https://guides.loc.gov/civil-war-soldiers/katharine-wormeley.

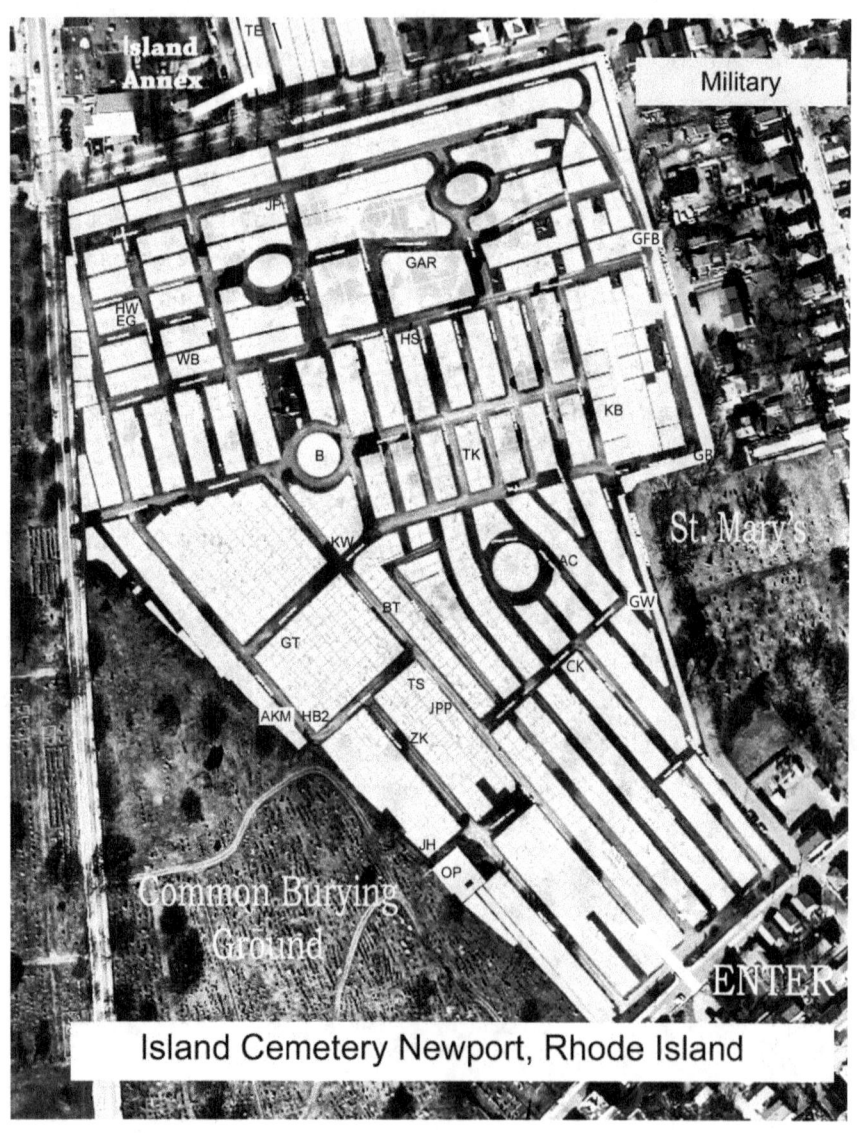

Island Cemetery Newport, Rhode Island

CHAPTER 5

Military Tour

For centuries, cemeteries have been places to honor the men and women of the military who served the country. Many died in battle at a young age while others were able to live a long life in the community after their service ended. This section is not intended to list every person who served and is buried in Island Cemetery. The individuals selected represent those who served and span time from the 1700s to 1900s.

Willett Clark Barrett

map WB

Barrett's grave stone states that he was born in Rochester, New York and a graduate of the University of Maine.[139] Barrett enlisted in Newport, Rhode Island to serve in WWI and achieved the rank of lieutenant. As commanding officer at-

Lt. Willett Clark Barrett
1895-1918

tached to Company G, 167th Infantry Regiment, 42nd Division, he was killed in action leading a charge at Hill 212 Sergy near Chateau Thierry in France. He was awarded a Purple Heart and a World War I Victory Medal.[140]

Perry Belmont
1851-1947

Perry Belmont

map B

Perry Belmont (1851-1947) was the oldest child of Caroline Slidell Perry Belmont and August Belmont. While known primarily as a United States politician, he served during the Spanish-American War as major and inspector general of the First Division, Second Army Corps, United States Volunteers.[141] He was the last surviving charter member of the Rhode Island Society of the Sons of the Revolution.[142]

---

[139]"The Role of Honor of the University of Maine," *The Bangor Daily News* (18 July 1918), 16.

[140] "Willett Clark Barrett," HonorStates.org, https://www.honorstates.org/index.php?id=577443

[141] Perry Belmont," *Biographical Directory of the United States Congress*, 1774-present, https://bioguideretro.congress.gov.

[142] "Perry Belmont, 96, Ex-Diplomat, Dead," *New York Times,* (26 May 1947), 1.

Gladys Carr Bolhouse
map GB

Gladys Bolhouse (1899-1995) was an important historian in the City of Newport for many years. Born in Newport, she attended Rogers High School. Following graduation in 1918, she joined the Navy as a Yeoman F.[143] Yeomen did administrative work and the designation of "F" was for female. These were the first women to enlist in the United States military, and their service in World War I was made possible by the Naval Act of 1916, which created a naval reserve force.

Chief Gunner George (F[144]) Patrick Brady
map GFB

Born in Ireland, George Brady (1867-1903) joined the United States Navy and served during the Spanish-American War. He was awarded a Congressional Medal of Honor for his valor. His citation reads:

> *"On board the torpedo Boat Winslow during the actions at Cardenas, Cuba, 11 May 1898. Conspicuously gallant during this period, Brady, by his energy in assisting to sustain fire, his efforts to repair the steering gear and his promptness in maintaining watertight integrity, was largely instrumental in saving the vessel."*[145]

The 1900 US Census indicates Brady was stationed at the Newport Torpedo Station. Three years later, he was on board the USS Monongahela when he died at the age of 36 from suicide. It was later found that shortly before the 6th of November 1903, Brady had stated that "the pain was unbearable," but it is unclear whether the pain was physical or psychological.[146]

---

[143] Richard Champlin (1995) "Tribute to Gladys Bolhouse," *Newport History*: Vol. 67: Issue 231, Article 4. Available at: https://digitalcommons.salve.edu/newporthistory/vol67/iss231/4.

[144] Some sources indicate his middle initial is an "F" but a "P" would be correct.

[145] "George F Brady," https://www.cmohs.org/recipients/george-f-brady.

[146] Https://www.talesofhonorpodcast.com/stories/george-f-brady.

Captain Kidder Randolph Breese

map KB

Kidder Breese (1831-1881) was appointed midshipman in 1847 and served in the Mexican-American War on the U.S.S. Saratoga. After passing his exams at the United States Naval Academy in 1852, he joined Perry's expedition to Japan from 1852-1854. He continued to rise through the ranks while serving in the Civil War, assisting with the capture of New Orleans. He put in the better part of his remaining years of service on different types of shore duty, including a stint as an instructor and later commandant at the USNA and as commander of the Newport Torpedo Station.[147]

Brevet Brigadier General Henry Brewerton

map HB2

Henry Brewerton (1801-1879) entered the United States Military Academy at the age of 12, the youngest cadet of any time, and graduated in 1819. He taught there for the two years following his graduation. Brewerton then supervised the building of various forts and the Cumberland Road. He served as superintendent of the U.S.M.A. at West Point from 1845-1852. From the time he left the academy until 1870, he was in charge of a number of engineering projects: construction of the defenses of Baltimore Harbor, the Delaware Point Lookout and Hampton Roads. He was made a colonel in 1864 and awarded the title of brevet brigadier-general in 1865 for his lifetime of service. He died in Wilmington, Delaware but was brought to back for burial next to his wife who had died in Newport.[148]

---

[147] "Obituary: Capt. Kidder Randolph Breese," *Boston Post* (14 September 1881), 1.

[148] "Obituary: Gen. Henry Brewerton" *New York Times* (18 April 1879), 5.

Rear Admiral Augustus Case

map AC

Augustus Case (1813-1893) was appointed midshipmen in 1828 and served on a ship before entering the United States Naval Academy in 1831. After graduation in 1834, he served on a number of ships for the Navy and was commissioned a lieutenant in 1842. He served in the Mexican-American War, aiding in the capture of three significant strongholds as well as holding off the Mexican Army for ten days with a force of just 25 men, which prevented the escape of General Santa Anna.

Case was made a commander in 1855, and in 1861 after the Civil War broke out, appointed captain of the fleet known as the North At-

lantic Blockading Squadron that captured forts up and down the Atlantic Coast.

Case climbed higher in rank when named captain in 1863, commodore in 1867, and rear admiral in 1872. He retired in 1875 having spent 25 years at sea and 12 years on shore duty. In 1880 he built a lovely house at 5 Catherine Street in Newport.[149]

---

[149] "Death of Admiral Case, U.S.N.," *Newport Mercury* (18 February 1893), 1.

Lieutenant Thomas Eadie, U.S.N

map TE

Thomas Eadie (1887-1974) was awarded the Medal of Honor from President Coolidge for using his diving skills to rescue a fellow Navy diver in 1927.

Thomas Eadie was born in Scotland in 1887. He enlisted in the United States Navy in by 1909 and became a gunner's mate but was also trained as a diver. While serving as a chief gunner's mate in the 1920s, he assisted in salvage work on the sunken submarines S-51 (SS-162) and S-4 (SS-109), receiving the Navy Cross for each operation, and the Medal of Honor for extraordinary heroism in rescuing a fellow diver on the S-4 on 18 December 1927. His award stated;

"For display of extraordinary heroism in the line of his profession above and beyond the call of duty on 18 December 1927, during the diving operations in connection with the sinking of the U.S.S. S-4 with all on board, as a result of a collision off Provincetown, Mass. On this occasion when MICHELS, Chief Torpedoman, United States Navy, while attempting to connect an airline to the submarine at a depth of 102 feet became seriously fouled, EADIE, under the most adverse diving conditions, deliberately, knowingly and willingly took his own life in his hands by promptly descending to the rescue in response to the desperate need of his companion diver. After two hours of extremely dangerous and heartbreaking work, by his cool, calculating and skillful labors, he succeeded in his mission and brought MICHELS safely to the surface."[150]

Eadie retired from active duty in 1939 but returned to service during World War II, receiving an appointment as chief gunner (warrant officer). He later became a commissioned officer and retired with the rank of lieutenant. Thomas Eadie died at Brockton, Massachusetts on November 14, 1974.[151]

---

[150] "Thomas Eadie," https://www.cmohs.org/recipients/thomas-eadie.
[151] Ibid.

Evanda B. Garnett

map HW

Garnett (1896-1918) was a native Newporter who, after graduating from Rogers High School, joined Light Battery A of the Rhode Island Militia and subsequently served in operations on the Mexican border in 1916.

Since he was unable to serve in the Aviation Section of the United States Army, Garnett applied to and was accepted into the Royal Flying Corps in Toronto, and after training, went to Northumberland, England. For a time, he was unable to fly because he suffered from migraines which kept him grounded, but he was ultimately cleared to fly in early 1918. On January 27th, he took off in an Avro 504J and had only flown about 100 feet when the plane crashed and burst into flames. He died later that day from his injuries.

The local paper in Newport reported erroneously that he had seen combat and downed four German planes, but Garnett was still training when he crashed. His ashes were buried in England. In 1959, his sister, Carole Garnett Wheeler, flew to London to request his ashes be exhumed and brought back for burial in Newport.[152]

---

[152] Nick Metcalfe, "Second Lieutenant Evanda Berkeley Garnett," *Sacrifice: Casualties of the Frist World War Commemorated by the Commonwealth War Graves Commission in the United States,* http://ww1sacrifice.com/2016/07/19/second-lieutenant-evanda-berkeley-garnett.

Grand Army of the Republic site

map GAR

This section of burials was established by the Grand Army of the Republic. The organization was a nationwide fraternity of veterans of the Civil War and was established in 1866. The organization ceased to exist in 1949, and ownership of this site went to the Sons of Union Veterans of the Civil War, an organization that was formed in 1881 but was an outgrowth of the GAR.[153]

Major John Handy

map JH

John Handy (1756-1828) moved to Newport and owned land south of the Old Stone Mill. He served during the American Revolution under Col. Archibald Crary.[154] On July 20, 1776 Handy read the newly-created Declaration of Independence to those gathered in front of the Colony House. In 1826, fifty years later, he reprised the reading of the document.

Theodore Wheaton King

map TK

Five days after the Civil War broke out, Newporter Theodore Wheaton King (1841-1862), signed up to serve in the Company F of the Newport Regiment for a period of three months. On July 21, 1861, he was shot in the hip/thigh during the first Battle of Bull Run. Left lying on the battlefield, King was taken to a Confederate prison hospital in Richmond, Virginia. The King family tried to get word on his condition

---

[153]"Sons of Union Veterans of the Civil War: About the SUVCW," https://www.suvcw.org/?page_id=6.

[154] U.S., Revolutionary War Rolls, 1775-1783, http://www.*Ancestry.com.*

and travelled to Richmond to try to find their son.[155] Infection and dysentery took their toll, and in February of 1862, on his way back to Newport, Theodore Wheaton King died in Philadelphia with his parents at his side.[156]

Theodore Wheaton King
1841-1862

William Vernon King

map CK

William King (1838-1864) was an officer who served in an all-Black regiment, defied his mother's antiwar stance by reenlisting, and was killed at Petersburg in 1864[157].

[155] Stensrud, 322.

[156] Article from folder 42 of the William Porcher Miles Papers #508, Southern Historical Collection, The Wilson Library, University of North Carolina at Chapel Hill. Https://web.lib.unc.edu/civilwar/index.php/2011/07/29/29-july-1861-2/

[157] Martha Sandweiss, *Passing Strange* (New York: Penguin Press, 2009), 28.

Zebulon King

map ZK

Zebulon King (1750-1789) was born and raised in Massachusetts. In 1778 he enlisted in the Fourth Massachusetts Regiment and served through 1783, becoming a lieutenant and finally a captain. He married Deborah Bird at Trinity Church in Newport, Rhode Island in 1784. As a soldier in the American Revolution, King was entitled to and applied for a land grant of 300 acres in Ohio. A few years after arriving there, Zebulon King was killed by Native Americans. Although his name appears on his wife's stone in Island Cemetery, he is actually buried in Ohio.[158]

In a somewhat ironic twist, King's only son, Charles Bird King, became an artist who specialized in painting portraits of Native Americans.

Andrew Kirk McMahon

map AKM

Andrew McMahon (1841-1921) was born in Northern Ireland, but his family came to the United States in 1845, where he spent most of his early life in Taunton, Massachusetts. After high school he worked as a day laborer.

In 1861 he enlisted with the 2nd Rhode Island Volunteers and fought in a number of battles through 1864. In May of that year, he was shot in the head during the Battle of Salem Heights in Virginia and was honorably discharged the following month.[159]

(Additional information about McMahon can be found in the Newportant tour)

---

[158] Herman J. Viola, *The Indian Legacy of Charles Bird King* (Washington, D.C.: Smithsonian Institution Press, 1976), 15.

[159] "Andrew K. McMahon," *Newport Mercury* (6 August 1921), 1.

John P Peckham

map JPP

John Peckham (1841-1861) was born in Newport. His father William was a carpenter according to the U.S. census. John enlisted in 1861 and was a private in Company F 1st Infantry. On July 21st he was killed at Bull Run, which is regarded by many as the first battle of the Civil War.[160]

Captain Christopher Raymond Perry

map B

Christopher Perry (1761-1818) was born in Kingston, Rhode Island and served during the American Revolution both on land and on sea.[161] His five sons later served the country in the United States Navy, the most famous being Oliver Hazard Perry and Matthew Calbraith Perry.

Captain Christopher Perry
1761-1818

Commodore Matthew C. Perry

map B

Perry (1794-1858) was born in South Kingston, Rhode Island. His father was active in the early United States Navy as was his brother, Oliver Hazard Perry. Matthew entered the Navy in 1809 and early in his career was stationed off the coast of Africa. He was involved in establishing the first settlement of free Blacks in Liberia. Perry was appointed to the Brooklyn Navy yard when not assigned overseas. His most distinguished service was

---

[160] "U.S., Civil War Soldier Records and Profiles, 1861-1865," https://www.*Ancestry.com*.

[161] Alexander Slidell Mackenzie, *"Commodore Oliver Hazard Perry: Famous American Naval Hero, Victor of the Battle of Lake Erie, His life and Achievements"*, (Akron, Ohio: The Superior Printing Company, 1915), 12.

the 1852-1854 expedition to Japan that opened trading with that country.[162]

Commodore Oliver Hazard Perry (1785-1819)

map OP

Oliver Hazard Perry (1785-1819) was born and raised in South Kingston, Rhode Island. At the age of 13, he was warranted a midshipman in the United States Navy, and later served during the Quasi-War with France and the Tripolitan War against the Barbary pirates. In 1809 he received his first command, the schooner Revenge. His fame resulted from his participation in the War of 1812. Perry directed the construction of a fleet on Lake Erie and engaged and defeated the British in battle. President Monroe sent Perry on a diplomatic mission to Venezuela in 1819. While there, he contracted yellow fever and died. [163]

John Hare Powel

map JP

John Hare Powel (1852-1892) was born in Paris, France to a well-established family from Philadelphia. The family summered in Newport and in 1860, Powel became a year-round Newport resident. In 1862 he enlisted as a captain but was soon promoted to major to serve in the Civil War in Company L, 9th Infantry.[164]

---

[162] "Death of Commodore M.C. Perry," *New York Times* (5 March 1858), 4.

[163] "Oliver Hazard Perry", *Naval History and Heritage Command website*, https://www.history.navy.mil/browse-by-topic/people/historical-figures/oliver-hazard-perry.html.

[164] "US Civil War Soldiers Records and Profiles," https://www.*Ancestry.com*.

Major General Thomas West Sherman

map TS

Sherman (1813-1879) was born in Newport and known to his friends as Tim. It is believed he walked from Newport to Washington D.C. to seek an appointment to West Point, which he received and from which he graduated in 1836.[165]   Sherman was later commissioned as a second lieutenant in the 3rd U.S. Artillery. He served during the Mexican-American War and the Civil War. In the May 27, 1863 attack on Port Hudson, Louisiana, he was severely wounded which led to the amputation of his leg. [166] It was reported in 1871 that Major General Thomas W. Sherman, commander of the Third Artillery had retired.

Brevet Brigadier General Hazard Stevens

map HS

Brevet Brigadier General Hazard Stevens
1842-1918

Hazard Stevens (1842-1918) was born in Newport, educated at Phillips Andover Academy and was a Harvard student when the Civil War began. He left school to serve in the War as first lieutenant and adjutant of the 79th New York Infantry. By 1861 he was promoted to captain and that same year, major. Stevens was wounded at the Battle of Chantilly and later wounded at the Battle of the Wilderness. He was mustered out of service

---

[165] "Retired", *Newport Mercury* (5 January 1871), 2.

[166] "Union General Thomas West Sherman," *Worthopdeia,* https://www.worthpoint.com/Worthopedia/cdv-union-general-thomas-west-sherman-291181920.

September 30, 1865, having twice been honored for gallantry and distinguished service. He received the Congressional Medal of Honor for his role in the capture of Fort Huger, Virginia. [167]

Major General Isaac Ingalls Stevens

map HS

Isaac Stevens (1818-1862) graduated from West point and served with distinction during the Mexican and Indian wars. He was serving as governor of Washington Territory when the Civil War broke out. Stevens resigned his position and was commissioned a colonel in the Union Army. He was killed in action during the Battle of Chantilly, September 1, 1862, the same battle in which his son, Hazard, was wounded. Hazard later wrote a biography of his father. [168]

Major General Isaac Stevens
1818-1862

Brevet Brigadier General George W. Tew

map GT

George Tew (1829-1884) was born and raised in Newport. At the age of 18 he joined the Newport Artillery Company where he worked his way up to commander by the start of the Civil War. In April, 1861 he was commissioned captain of the First RI Militia and later captain of the Fourth Regiment and eventually promoted to lieutenant colonel. He resigned on August 11, 1862, and by October was commissioned as major in the 6th Heavy Artillery Regiment. He was later promoted to colonel and placed in command of Fort Torren in North Carolina.[169]

---

[167]"General Hazard Stevens," *Newport Journal and Weekly News* (18 October 1918), 1.

[168] "The Grist Mill," *Newport Daily News* (15 February 1957), 6.

[169] "Col. George W. Tew," *Newport Mercury* (15 November 1884), 1.

George Tiffany

map B

George Tiffany (1896-1946) was born in New York to Belmont and Ann Tiffany. He was a student at Harvard when war was declared in 1917. He was commissioned as a lieutenant in the Aviation Corps and reached France with the first wave of American flyers. He and five other flyers were shot down and spent months in a German prison camp before escaping. He served during WWII and attained the rank of lieutenant colonel.[170]

William Tiffany

map B

WILLIAM TIFFANY
1868-1898

William Tiffany (1868-1898) was born in Newport, later moved in the highest social circles of New York, and was always impeccably attired. He, like many in his social set, heeded the call for volunteers to join Roosevelt's Rough Riders and served in the Spanish-American War. He took part in the Battle of Las Guasimas, the Battle of San Juan Hill, and the Siege of Santiago de Cuba. Tiffany took ill while serving and was transported to Boston where his condition worsened, and he died in the Parker House surrounded by family members and his fiancé.[171]

> *"I am greatly shocked and grieved at poor young Tiffany's death. He was one of the most gallant and efficient officers we had, a man of dauntless courage and absorbed attention to duty. I grew to rely on him more and more, and all of us will mourn him both as a staunch friend and tried comrade-in-arms. There is a peculiar element of sadness in the fate of*

---

[170] "George Tiffany, 50, Found Dead in Bed," *New York Times* (29 November 1946), 25.

[171] "Lieutenant Tiffany Dead," *New York Times* (26 August 1898), 2.

these young fellows, who have reached the shore for which they longed only to die." Colonel Theodore Roosevelt

Commodore Benjamin J. Totten

map BT

Totten (1806-1877) was born in the West Indies and entered the Navy as a midshipman in 1823. He was promoted to lieutenant in 1834 and commissioned as a commander in 1855. From 1858-1860 he was in charge of a sloop stationed off the coast of Africa to suppress the slave trade. During the Civil War he was stationed at Hampton Roads, Virginia and was promoted to commodore in 1864. From 1867-1869 he served as governor of the Naval Asylum in Philadelphia. Totten was the author of *Totten's Naval Text-Book* first published in 1841. [172]

Major General Gouverneur K. Warren

map GW

Warren (1830-1882) graduated second in his class from West

Major General Gouverneur Warren
1830-1882

Point in 1850. Commissioned into the Corps of Topographical Engineers, he spent years mapping the western part of the United States with a focus on the Mississippi River. He was appointed a lieutenant colonel at the outbreak of the Civil War and saw action in a number of battles before commanding a brigade at the Battle of the Second Manassas and the Battle of Antietam. For his service he was promoted to Brigadier General of Volunteers. His fame was earned at Gettysburg where he identified

---

[172] "Benjamin J. Totten," *Appleton's Cyclopedia of American Biography, 1600-1889*. Vol VI, 140, https://www.Ancestry.com.

the importance of a strategic position, Little Round Top, that was un-
guarded and would lead to the outflanking of the Union forces. Warren took action to man the site, and the defense of the hill was vital
in the victory. For his actions he was promoted to major general[173]. A
statue stands on the hill in dedication to his leadership with the following dedication:

Led to this spot
by his military sagacity on July 2, 1863
General Gouverneur Kemble Warren
then Chief Engineer of the Army of the Potomac
detected General Hood's flanking movement
and by promptly assuming the responsibility of
ordering troops to this place saved the key
of the Union position.

Promoted for gallant services
from the command of a regiment in 1861, through
successive grades to the command of the 2nd Army
Corps in 1863, and permanently assigned to that
of the 5th Army Corps in 1864.
Major General Warren needs no eulogy.
His name is enshrined in the hearts of his countrymen.

This statue
is erected under the auspices of the veteran
organization of his old regiment, the 5th New York
Vols. Duryee Zouaves in memory of their beloved
commander.

Dedicated August 8th 1888

---

[173] "Gouverneur K. Warren," https://www.battlefields.org/learn/biog-
raphies/gouverneur-k-warren

Frank Leslie's illustration depicting a Memorial Day tribute to Warren by members of the Fifth New York Volunteer Veteran Association, 1887

Warren monument at Gettysburg

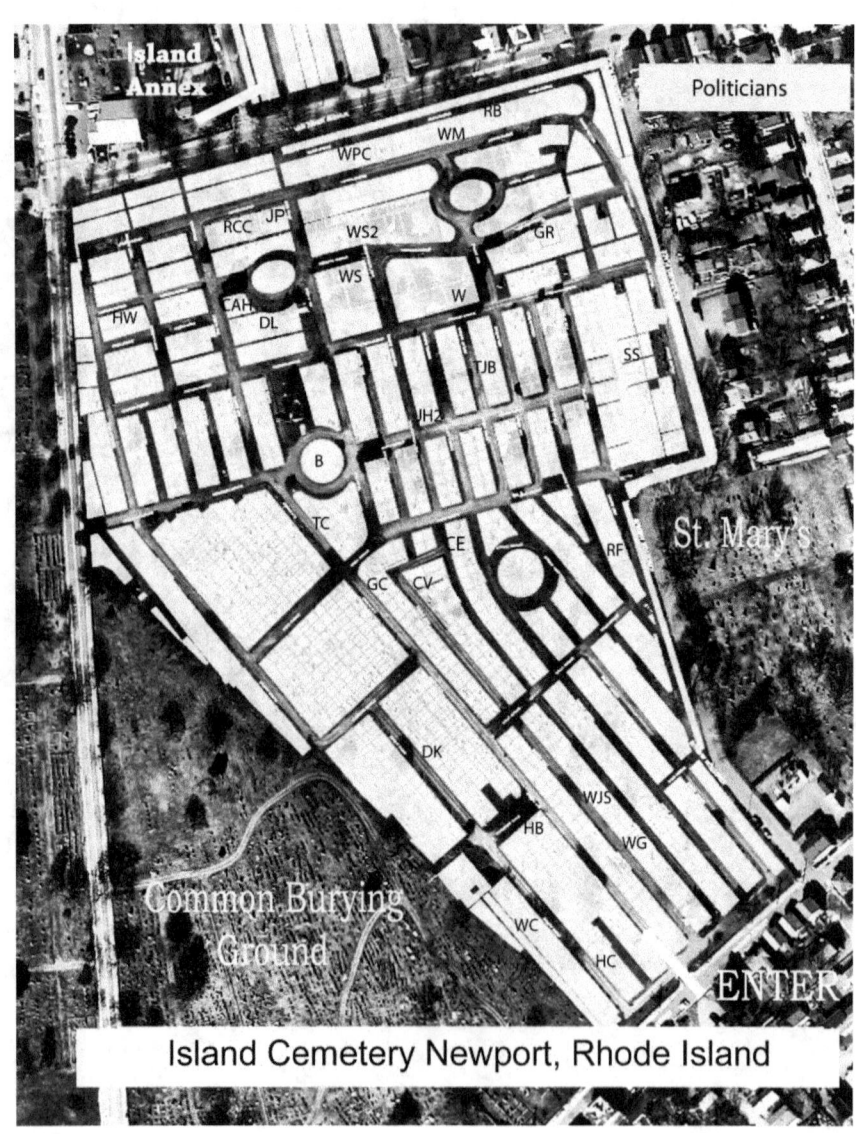

Island Cemetery Newport, Rhode Island

CHAPTER 6

Notable Politicians

Henry Bedlow

map JH2

Henry Bedlow (1821-1914) was born to an old Knickerbocker family that owned the land that is now Ellis Island in New York Harbor. He was educated at Yale and Harvard, where he studied medicine. He became the owner of Malbone Hall when he married in 1850. Bedlow was elected mayor of Newport in 1875[174] and served until 1879.

HON. HENRY BEDLOW, MAYOR OF NEWPORT, R.I.

---

[174] "Death of Henry Bedlow," *Newport Daily News* (1 June 1914), 1.

J Truman Burdick

map TJB

Burdick (1839-1908) was born in Newport, attended local schools and joined his father in business in the building trades. He enlisted to serve during the Civil War in the 9th Rhode Island Regiment and started a grocery business when he returned from the war. Burdick served as mayor 1879-1880, served on city council and was a founding member of the Newport Street Railway, but he was best known for his charitable efforts. It seems ironic that his death occurred when he was hit by a street car at Broadway and Mann.[175]

Perry Belmont

map B

Belmont (1851-1947) was the United States Minister to Spain in 1898 and served as the New York Representative to Congress 1881-

1888. For a time, he lived at Belcourt Castle in Newport, the house his brother, OHP Belmont, had built. Perry sold the property in 1941 and had the statue of his father, August Belmont, moved to Washington Square. Belmont also sponsored the relocation of the Rochambeau statue from Broadway to King Park.[176]

---

[175] "J Truman Burdick Killed," *Newport Mercury,* (24 October 1908), 1.
[176] "Perry Belmont, 96, Former Diplomat, Dies," *Newport Mercury* (30 May 1947), 1.

Robert S Burlingame

map RB

Burlingame (1864-1945) served as postmaster and as mayor of Newport in 1915. He was a representative to the state legislature and served 3 consecutive terms.[177]

Melville Bull

map HB

Bull (1854-1909) was a Rhode Island Representative to the U.S. Congress 1895-1903. He also served as a state senator, state representative, and lieutenant governor. Bull was the youngest son of Henry Bull and was educated in Newport and Phillips Exeter Academy. He never married, was active in public service and social clubs and made many friends.[178]

George Henry Calvert

map GC

Calvert (1803-1889) served as mayor of Newport 1853-1854 but is more widely known as an editor, essayist, dramatist and biographer. He was the great-grandson of Lord Baltimore.

---

[177] "Robert S. Burlinger, Former Mayor, Dies," *Newport Mercury* (2 November 1945), 3.

[178] "Recent Deaths- Ex-congressman Bull," *Newport Mercury* (10 July 1909), 1.

William Pratt Clarke

map **WPC**

Clarke (1870-1937) graduated from Rogers High School, went west to work on a ranch and then returned to Newport to work in his father's news and stationery store on Thames Street. Clarke served five terms as the Newport representative to the state government starting in 1906 and was an active member of the school committee. He is credited with helping to develop championship basketball teams in the city.[179] He served as mayor of Newport 1907-08.

Thomas Coggeshall

map TC

Coggeshall (1829-1900) served as mayor of Newport 1889-1891. In addition, he served 20 years as a board member of the State Charity Commission and 25 years as president of Aquidneck National Bank. He was instrumental in opening the Wickford to New York Rail Line and having Ocean Drive laid out.[180]

Robert Clarke Cottrell

map RCC

Cottrell (1853-1932) was an undertaker in Newport for 60 years and active in Trinity Church for more than four decades. In 1905 he defeated incumbent Patrick Boyle for mayor.[181]

---

[179] "William P. Clarke, Former Mayor, Dead," *Newport Mercury* (3 September 1937), 1.

[180] "T.C. Elected without Opposition," *New York Times* (21 September 1888), 5.

[181] "Many at Funeral of Robert C. Cottrell," *Newport Mercury* (22 January 1932), 6.

William Cole Cozzens

map WC

Cozzens (1811-1876) served as mayor of Newport (1865-1855), state representative and senator, and briefly as governor when Governor Sprague resigned to become a U.S. Senator. He later ran for election to the post but lost.

Henry Young Cranston

map HC

Henry Cranston (1789-1864) served as the Rhode Island Representative to the U.S. Congress 1843-1847. Prior to 1843 he was the Speaker of the House in Rhode Island (1839-1840).

William H. Cranston

map HC

William H. Cranston (1821-1871) served as mayor of Newport 1857-1866. He was the son of former Mayor H.Y. Cranston.

Robert Bennie Cranston

map HC

Robert Cranston (1791-1873) was born in Newport and served the city as revenue collector (1812-1815), sheriff (1821-1827), postmaster (1827), state representative (1843-1847) and U.S. congressman (1837-1843). His obituary stated he left $75,000 to the poor and was "too honest to steal and too proud to beg."[182] Cranston was elected mayor in 1853 but declined the position. He was the brother of Henry Cranston, one of the initial trustees of Island Cemetery.

Christopher Ellery

map CE

Ellery (1768-1840) served as a U.S. senator from Rhode Island. He was the nephew of William Ellery, signer of the Declaration of independence.

William Channing Gibbs

map WG

Gibbs (1787-1871) was born in Newport, educated at Harvard, served as governor of Rhode Island (1821-1824) and a representative to the state from Newport (1816-1820). He sold the land that became Touro Park and included the stone tower to the city in 1851.[183] His obituary describes him as honorable, generous and kind.[184]

---

[182] "Obituary: Robert B. Cranston," *New York Times* (28 January 1873), 1.

[183] "Touro Park Memorial for Its Donors Planned," *Newport Daily News* (26 April 1951), 1.

[184] "Death of Governor Gibbs," *Newport Daily News* (21 February 1871), 2.

Robert Stillman Franklin

map RF

Robert Franklin (1836-1913) was the son of a baker and joined the bakery at the corner of Spring Street and Mary Street. In addition to being a devoted family man, active in fraternal organizations and a volunteer firefighter, he served the city in many elected positions. Franklin was mayor (1882-1885) and served for 10 years on Newport City Council.[185]

Charles A Hambly

map CAH

The Hambly family moved to Newport when Charles (1916-2008) was 2 years old. He later served as a member of city council and mayor (1961-1965). He was vice-chair of the Newport Redevelopment Agency, which was integral to the work being done along the harbor. In 1974 he sold the funeral home that bears the family name. Hambly was an active member of the Lions Club for 75 years, president of the Chamber of Commerce, and co-chair of the YMCA Building Fund.[186]

George Gordon King

map DK

George King (1807-1870) was the oldest son of Dr. David King and Ann Gordon. After being educated at Phillips Andover Academy, Brown University and Litchfield Law School, he entered politics. King served in the legislature of Rhode Island 1845, 1846, and from 1849-1853 was the Rhode Island Representative to the U.S. Congress.

---

[185] "Robert S. Franklin," *Newport Mercury* (11 October 1913), 1.
[186] "Charles A. Hambly," https://memorialfuneralhome.com/obituary/470263/charles-a.-hambly/obituary-services

Lt. Colonel John Hare Powel Jr.

map JP

Powel (1837-1908) was born in Paris to a prominent Philadelphia family who summered in Newport, but the city became his permanent home in 1860. Powel served his country during the Civil War and his city as mayor (1886-1888) and Rhode Island as a state senator. He was active in the Newport Reading Room, the Redwood Library and president and trustee of the Newport Hospital. Powel was described as charitable with high integrity and an interest in the city.[187]

Dean J Lewis

map DL

Lewis (1916-1997) was born in Boston and educated at Harvard and Harvard Law School. He served in the Navy with J.F. Kennedy where he commanded PT183. He retired from the Navy in 1945 and served as mayor of Newport 1950-1954. He was instrumental in getting federal money for the development of the former Naval Supply Depot and the Naval Piers in Newport. Lewis was active in a number of fraternal organizations and St. Spyridon Church.[188]

William MacLeod

map WM

MacLeod (1883-1960) was a graduate of Rogers High School, Harvard and Harvard Law School. He served the country during WWI and was the youngest man elected mayor of Newport in 1913 at the age of 29. He led the effort for Newport to get control of the waterworks. MacLeod was an active mountain climber, hiker, actor, and member

---

[187] "John Hare Powel," *Newport Mercury* (4 January 1908), 1.
[188] "Dean J. Lewis, Former Mayor, Gubernatorial Candidate," *Providence Journal* (11 November 1997), B-04.

of the United Congregational Church, the Newport Historical Society and the Newport Art Association.[189]

George Lockhart Rives

map GR

While Rives (1849-1917) was not elected to any position, he traveled in political circles and served as the Assistant Secretary of State for the United States during the Grover Cleveland Administration. He was also a trustee of the New York Public Library, Columbia University and New York Hospital.

William Sheffield, Jr.

William Sheffield, Sr.

William Paine Sheffield Jr

map WS2

W.P. Sheffield, Jr (1857-1919) was born in Newport, educated at Phillips Andover Academy, Brown University, Harvard Law and in Paris. He was active on the school committee and a board member of the Newport Historical Society. As a director of the Savings Bank of Newport, he was also a member of a number of boards

---

[189] "Ex-mayor William MacLeod Dies, Lawyer, Veteran Was School Head," *Newport Daily News* (2 July 1960), 1.

including Emmanuel Church, the Newport Water Works, trustee of Long Wharf, Brown University and the Fall River Street Railway.[190]

William Paine Sheffield Sr.

map WS

W.P. Sheffield, Sr (1820-1907) was born on Block Island and educated at the Kingston Academy and Harvard Law. He was a delegate to the State Constitution Convention in 1841-1842 and elected to the state legislature 1842-1845, 1849-1853, and 1857-1861. Sheffield was appointed senator from Rhode Island to Washington upon the death of Henry B. Anthony and served from 1884-1885. He was the President of the Trustees of the Peoples Library and served on the boards of the Rhode Island Historical Society and the Newport Historical Society.[191]

Stephen P. Slocum

map SS

Slocum (1818-1902) served Newport in a number of positions. He was mayor 1880-1882, an alderman and a member of the school committee.

William J Swinburne

map WJS

Swinburne (1823-1897) was born in Newport and served during the Mexican-American War (1846-1849). He was mayor (1855-1857) during the "Know Nothing excitement", a volunteer firefighter and school committee member for 15 years.[192]

---

[190] "William P. Sheffield," *Newport Mercury* (25 October 1919), 1.
[191] "William P. Sheffield," *Newport Mercury* (8 June 1907), 1.
[192] "William J Swinburne; Death of One of Newport's Early Mayors and a Mexican War Veteran," *Newport Daily News* (20 September 1897), 7.

Charles Collins Van Zandt

map CV

Van Zandt (1830-1894) was born in Newport into an old Knickerbocker family. After graduating from Trinity College, he served as city
solicitor in 1855, state legislator in 1857 (where he served as Speaker
of the House), state senator 1869-1870, lt. governor 1873-1875 and
governor 1877-1880. He is credited with improving the Rhode Island
education system.[193]

---

[193] "Ex-Governor Van Zandt Dead," *Newport Mercury* (9 June 1894), 1.

George Peabody Wetmore

map W

Wetmore (1846-1921) was born in London, educated in Newport and at Yale and Columbia Law School. He was a member of the commission that oversaw the construction of a new state house in Providence, chairman of the committee that completed the U.S. Capitol Building, chairman of the Lincoln Memorial Commission and a member of the Grant Memorial Commission. In addition, he was a trustee of the Peabody Museum of Natural History, an organizer of the Metropolitan Opera, a founding member of the Jockey Club, and vice-president of the National Horse Show Association of America. Locally Wetmore was a trustee of the Redwood Library, president and trustee of the Newport Hospital and the Newport Casino.

He was the 37th governor of the state, serving from 1885-1887, and U.S. Senator from Rhode Island 1895-1907.

Wetmore and his family lived in Chateau-sur-Mer, the estate he inherited from his father and had remodeled by Richard Morris Hunt.[194]

[194]"George P. Wetmore, Governor, U.S. Senator,"
  https://www.geni.com/people/George-P-Wetmore-Governor-U-S-Senator

Henry S. Wheeler

map HW

Wheeler (1894-1967) served as mayor of Newport from 1935-1940. He was a veteran of WWI, WWII, and Korea. Born in Akron, Ohio, his life in Newport started in 1898. He graduated from Rogers High School and George Washington University. In 1935 he joined the editorial staff of the Newport Daily News. In addition to his time as mayor, Wheeler also served on the school committee (1936, 1938), was director of the Chamber of Commerce, Newport Red Cross, Newport YMCA and the American Legion.[195]

---

[195] "Col. Wheeler Dies," *Newport Daily News* (1 August 1967), 1.

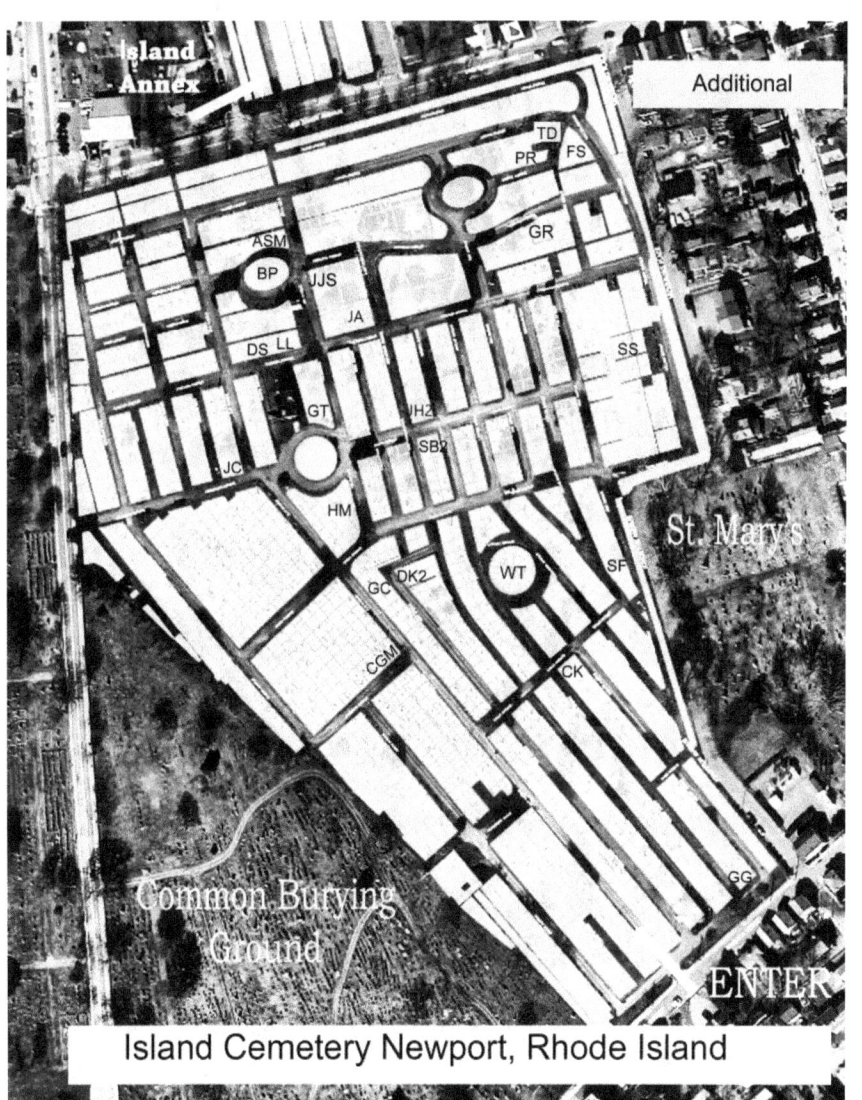

Island Cemetery Newport, Rhode Island

Chapter 7

Additional Notable Burials in Island Cemetery

Hugh D. Auchincloss

map JA

Hugh D. Auchincloss Jr. (1897-1976) was born at Hammersmith Farm in 1897 to a merchant and financier. He attended the Groton School, Yale, and Columbia University, where he obtained a degree in Law. He practiced law for two years before joining two different federal departments in Washington as an aviation expert.

In 1931, he formed a brokerage firm and bought a seat on the New York Stock Exchange. During World War II, he served with U.S. Naval Intelligence.

He was married three times. His first wife was a Russian noblewoman, Maya de Chrapovitsky. They had one son, Hugh D. "Yusha" Auchincloss III, and divorced in 1932. Next, he married Nina Vidal, mother of author Gore Vidal, and they had two more children before divorcing in 1941.

In 1942 he married Lee Bouvier and became stepfather to Jacquelin and Lee Bouvier. He reportedly got Jacquelin her first job with the *Washington Times Herald.* He also walked her down the aisle when she married Senator John F. Kennedy in Newport in 1953 and hosted the wedding reception for the couple at Hammersmith Farm.

Auchincloss was a philanthropist who supported the Boys Club of Newport County and the Boys Club of America as well as serving as a member of both boards. He was also on the board of directors of the Redwood Library. He was a member of many clubs in both New York and Washington and a member of the Masonic Lodge.[196]

Janet and Hugh Auchincloss

---

[196] Thomas W. Ennis, "Hugh Auchincloss Sr., Stockbroker, Dead," *New York Times* (22 November 1976), 38.

Seth Bateman

map SB2

Seth Bateman (1802-1887) was born in the house that he later transformed into a summer hostelry, Bateman House, an establishment enjoyed by American and European guests of the highest social circles. He was one of 12 children of William and Susannah Bateman. Bateman married and had one child who died soon after he was born. Bateman was a hard-working member of the Newport's Quaker community who served as president of the Merchants Bank. When Bateman died, there was speculation that part of the Bateman fortune would be left to Seth Bateman Dodge, a protégé of Seth Bateman, but Dodge had been involved in an 1878 scandal in which he eloped with the daughter of a guest at the hotel so he received nothing from the will. A nephew, W. Sidney Bateman, assumed operation of the hotel following his uncle's death.[197] In 1959 the building was lost due to fire.

George Henry Calvert

map GC

Calvert (1803-1889) was born in Prince George's County, Maryland. He was a direct descendant of the founder of the Colony of Maryland. Calvert was educated at Harvard and the University of Gottingen in Germany. He moved to Newport in 1843 and was later elected mayor. He is considered a man of letters, poet, dramatist, travel writer, art critic, translator, and biographer. Ralph Waldo Emerson, Edgar Allen Poe and Henry Wadsworth Longfellow were among his acquaintances.[198] In addition, Calvert was the president of the Perry Monument Association.[199]

---

[197] "Death of Seth Bateman," *Newport Mercury* (5 November 1887), 1.

[198] John R. Shook, "George Henry Calvert (1803-89)," *The Dictionary of Modern American Philosophers*, published online isbn9780199754663, 2010.

[199] "Perry Monument Association," *New York Times* (14 January 1883), 9.

John Rose Caswell

map JC

Caswell (1834-1918) was born in Jamestown, Rhode Island and was the son of Captain Philip Caswell and Elizabeth Rose Caswell. He is listed as a druggist in the 1860 Federal Census and in 1859 had joined

his brother Phillip in the firm of Caswell, Hazard and Company, which was established in 1867. In 1876 Caswell formed a partnership with William Massey and the firm of Caswell, Massey & Company was established.[200] The firm continues to this day.

---

[200] "Caswell, Massey & Co. and Their Lengthy History," *Newport Mercury* (9 July 1887), 3.

Theodore Montgomery Davis

map TD

Davis (1837-1915) was American lawyer and businessman known for excavations in Egypt's Valley of the Kings from 1902 to 1913.

He was born in Springfield, New York and in 1882 moved to Newport, where he built his estate. For 30 years Davis owned the Reef, his estate on Ocean Avenue that today is part of Brenton Point State Park.

Davis was known as an Egyptologist who in 1905 excavated in the Valley of the Kings of Thebes and discovered the tombs of Queen Teie and later excavated the tomb of King Amen-hotep. Davis paid for his explorations and employed 150 men each season. His Newport home included relics of ancient Egypt.

Davis died in Florida at the estate of Secretary of State, William Jennings Bryan.[201] His private collection of Egyptian artifacts went to the Metropolitan Museum of Art in New York after his death.

---

[201] "Theodore M. Davis, Egyptologist, Dead," *New York Times*, (24 February 1915), 9.

George Washington Greene

map GG

George Washington Greene (1811-1883) was the grandson of Revolutionary War officer, Nathaniel
Green. Born in East Greenwich, RI in
1811, he was later educated at Brown
University and served as United States
consul in Italy. He began teaching modern languages at Brown in 1847, and in
1872 he was a professor of American
history at Cornell University. He was a
major contributor of articles to the
*North American Review, The Christian
Review, Knickerbocker Magazine, Harper's Magazine* and *Putnam's Magazine*. In addition, he wrote "The Life of

General Greene" and other texts for the instruction of the French and
Italian languages.[202]

---

[202] "Professor Greene Dead," *The Boston Globe* (3 February 1883), 1.

Jonathan Prescott Hall

map JH2

J. Prescott Hall (1796-1862), originally from Pomfret, Connecticut, was a leading lawyer of his time. At the request of President Zachary Taylor, he took the position of United States District Attorney for the Southern District of New York.[203]

In 1849, Hall hired architect Alexander Jackson Davis to build a Gothic Revival mansion directly on the ruins of Godfrey Malbone's estate on Malbone Road in Newport.[204]

Hall's grave stone has a classical pediment with an Egyptian Revival winged sun disk as a symbol of eternity, the soul and protection.[205]

---

[203] "Death of J. Prescott Hall," *New York Times* (30 September 1862), 8.

[204] "Malbone Mansion," *http://wikimapia.org/18441720/Malbone-Mansion-J-Prescott-Hall-Henry-Bedlow-House.*

[205] Island Cemetery Records, https://cemeteryfind.com/PublicSearch/BurialSearch/40d4b48a-189b-4a8c-b894-c31f0c90e100

Delancey Astor Kane

map DK2

Kane (1844-1915) was born in Newport and later graduated from West Point Military Academy. He studied at Trinity College in Cambridge, England and graduated from Columbia Law School in 1873.

Kane was active in civic affairs and served as an alderman in Newport. He was very enthusiastic about coaching, the sport with carriages and horses, and is credited with starting the sport in America. He was also an avid yachtsman and served as president of the New York Yacht Club.[206]

COACHING IN AMERICA—START OF COLONEL DELANCEY KANE'S NEW ROCHELLE AND PELHAM COACH FROM THE HOTEL BRUNSWICK, MADISON SQUARE.
[FROM A SKETCH BY OUR SPECIAL ARTIST.]

---

[206] "One of Three Who Came Often to Lenox; Kane Brothers Well Remembered There- Delancey Kane Was a Noted Horseman," *The Berkshire Eagle* (5 April 1915), 9.

Clarence King

map CK

Clarence King (1842-1901) was born in Newport to James Rivers King and Florence (Little) King. James King was in the China Trade and died in China when Clarence was just six, so Clarence was brought up primarily by his mother and his grandmother, Sophia Little, a strong abolitionist. After King's mother married again, his stepfather sent him to the Sheffield Scientific School, which was connected to Yale. He studied geography and decided on a career in the field.

In 1862, King traveled to the West to do geological surveys, sometimes without pay. His surveys, as well as those of others, were consolidated in 1879 by the U.S. Congress to create the United States Geological Survey. King was chosen as its first director and held that position for about two years.[207]

King joined a number of social clubs in New York and entertained members with his stories of life in the West. He was a real star of the Gilded Age, but his lavish lifestyle caused him to accrue great debt. In a bizarre twist, King assumed the identity of James Todd, an African American steelworker and Pullman porter who lived with his African American common law wife, Ada Copeland, and their five children in Brooklyn. He managed to keep his real identity a secret from her, and his family a secret from his New York society acquaintances. Just before his death in Arizona, King wrote a letter to Ada confessing the truth about his identity. He is buried in Newport next to his mother.[208]

---

[207] Robert Wilson, *The Explorer King: Adventure, Science, and the Great Diamond Hoax-Clarence King in the Old West* (New York: Scribner, 2006).

[208] Martha A. Sandweiss, *Passing Strange* (New York: Penguin Press, 2009).

Lewis Cass Ledyard

map LL

Born in Detroit, Ledyard (1851-1932) later attended Harvard University and Harvard Law School. After joining a prestigious law firm in New York City, he was counsel for the United States Steel Corporation and the American Tobacco Company as well as personal counsel for J. Pierpont Morgan. He was responsible for drafting and executing Morgan's will and those of Payne Whitney, Col. John Jacob Astor and William K. Vanderbilt among others.

In New York he was president of the New York Public Library, president of the Bar Association of the City of New York, a trustee of the Metropolitan Museum of Art and a member of many, many clubs. In his will Lewis Cass Ledyard left bequests to all these organizations including a $2 million gift to the New York Public Library.

Ledyard spent summers at his Newport estate, Sunset Ridge, on Ridge Road. He was a member of the Newport Reading Room and held many shares in the Newport Casino since its founding in 1881. He was a director of the Newport Country Club and one-time Commodore of the New York Yacht Club. Two years before his death he

gave $600,000 to Newport Hospital in memory of his father, Henry Ledyard, a founder and first president of the hospital.[209]

L.C. Ledyard died in New York, and after an elaborate funeral was brought to Newport by special train for burial in Island Cemetery.

---

[209] "Lewis Cass Ledyard Is Dead in New York," *Newport Mercury* (29 January 1932), 2.

Henry G. Marquand

map HM

Marquand (1819-1902) acquired his vast wealth through investments in New York City real estate and later established himself as a banker on Wall Street. He made a fortune speculating on foreign currency and on railroads. His railroad investments were bought out by Jay Gould in 1880, and Marquand decided to take his millions and retire.

Marquand was one of fifty men who met to establish the Metropolitan Museum of Art in New York and served as the head of the institute's Board of Trustees and later its second president. During his lifetime he donated an enormous amount of money to the museum as well as pieces from his personal art collection. He endowed Princeton University with the money to build a library and a chapel. His son became the first Art History professor at Princeton after his graduation from the school.

In 1873 Marquand hired Richard Morris Hunt to design a summer cottage called Linden Gate at the corner of Old Beach Road and Rhode Island Avenue. Hunt later designed a New York mansion for Marquand as well. Linden Gate burned down in 1973, and all that remains on the site is a gatehouse.

During his time in Newport, Marquand was a member of Julia Ward Howe's "Town and Country Club," a group of artists and intellectuals. The club ultimately led to the creation of the Newport Art Association, now known as the Newport Art Museum.

Elizabeth Allen Marquand died in 1895 and Henry Marquand died in 1902 at his home in New York City. He and his wife are buried in the tomb designed by Richard Morris Hunt.[210]

Bud Palmer

map BP

Bud Palmer (1921-2013) gained fame as a sportscaster, served as New York Mayor John Lindsay's official greeter, wrote a column for *Glamour Magazine,* and was the first captain of the New York Knicks basketball team. He was one of the first players to shoot a jump shot in basketball. Palmer tried out for the Knicks in 1946 and in three seasons averaged 11.7 points per game and 14.4 in playoff games.

Palmer was born John Shove Flynn in Hollywood, California. His parents divorced, and his mother, Blanche Palmer, and children changed their last name to her maiden name. The family spent time in Switzerland and in Princeton New Jersey, where he later enrolled in Princeton University after graduating from Phillips-Exeter Academy. He left college to enlist in the Navy as a pilot. Following three seasons as a basketball player, his career in television started as well as his career as in journalism[211].

---

[210] "Henry G. Marquand Dead," *New-York Tribune* (27 February 1902), 5; "Linden Gate, Old Beach Road, Newport, Newport County, RI;" Paul Miller, 40-42.

[211] Frank Litsky, "Bud Palmer, Jump Shot Pioneer Dies at 91," *New York Times* (22 March 2013), B8.

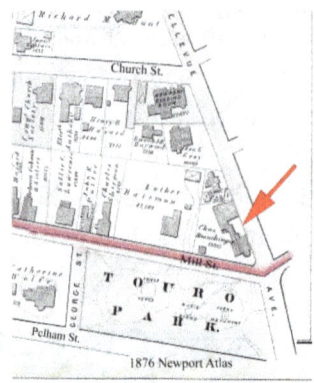

1876 Newport Atlas

Charles Gottlieb Muenchinger

map CGM

Muenchinger (1827-1898) was born in Germany and arrived in Norwich, Connecticut in 1848 with his wife Pauline. The couple moved to Newport in 1852[212] and became the leading confectioners in the city. By 1889 the business expanded to include catering with the help of their four sons. A large home and business appear on the 1876 Newport Atlas at the corner of Bellevue Avenue and Mill Street.

Gustave Adolf and Amanda S. Muenchinger (1854-1915),

map ASM

Gustave was one son of Charles Muenchinger, worked in the family business and later married Amanda Stratemann (1854- 1921) about 1884. She immigrated from Germany to the United Sates in 1875. The 1875 Rhode Island Census lists her as a single woman boarding in the Muenchinger home and working as a clerk. Accounts state that her husband, Gustave, joined her in managing the cottage business she started.[213] Their most significant achievement was turning the former home of Dr. David King on Bellevue Avenue into one of the most fashionable boarding houses in the city. Known as the Muenchinger-King House, it was the place "acceptable" visitors to the city stayed and also the site of celebrations and events for Newport citizens.

---

[212] "Death of Charles G Muenchinger," *Newport Mercury* (7 January 1889), https://www. *Ancestry.com*.

[213] "Mrs. Amanda S. Muenchinger," *Newport Mercury* (22 January 1921), 1.

Philip Mercer Rhinelander

map PR

Born in Newport to a very wealthy family, Rhinelander (1869-1939) went on to attend Harvard and Oxford University. After his ordination in 1896, he was put in charge of St Mark's Church in Washington, D.C. He taught at both Berkeley Divinity School in Connecticut and the Episcopal Theological Seminary in Cambridge, Massachusetts. In 1911 he became Bishop of the Diocese of Pennsylvania and served until 1923 when he retired due to ill health. He went back to teaching but died at his summer home in Gloucester, Massachusetts in 1939. His body was returned to Newport for burial in Island Cemetery.[214]

---

[214] "P.M. Rhinelander, Bishop, Dies at 70," *New York Times* (22 September, 1939), 30.

George Lockhart Rives

map GR

George Rives (1849-1917) received a law degree from Columbia

Law School and began practicing law in the 1870s in New York City. In 1887, President Grover Cleveland appointed him Assistant Secretary of State in charge of Latin Affairs, and he served in that post for two years. He practiced law for the rest of his life.

In New York, Rives was a director of the Bank of New York and the United States Trust Company. He was also a trustee of Columbia University and chairman of that board from 1903 until his death. He served on the boards of the New York Public Library, the Metropolitan Opera House and the New York County Bar Association as well. His name was proposed as a candidate for mayor of New York, but he refused to enter politics.

After the death of his first wife, Rives married Sarah Swan Whiting, who was divorced from OHP Belmont. Rives adopted Natica, the daughter Sarah had with Belmont. During summers, the couple resided first in Swanhurst on Bellevue Avenue and then at what is now known as Stargazer House on Narragansett Avenue.

In Newport, Rives served on the boards of both the Newport Historical Society and the Newport Casino, and he was instrumental in the formation of the Spouting Rock Beach Association.[215]

---

[215]"George L. Rives, Noted Lawyer, Dies," *New York Times* (19 August 1917), 15.

Eileen Gillespie Slocum

Map JJS

Born in New York City (1915-2008), she was the granddaughter of John Carter Brown. A broken engagement to John Jacob Astor V was followed by marriage to John Jermain Slocum, journalist and diplomat. Eileen Slocum was viewed by many as the last of the Newport Grande Dames and achieved national recognition for her support of the Republican Party. She exhibited impeccable manners, refined elegance, had strong opinions, was quick-witted and had an impressive memory. Her home at 459 Bellevue Avenue was the epicenter of Newport society for decades.[216] Her life was the subject of a film in 2010 called "Behind the Hedgerow."

Frank K. Sturgis

Map FS

Sturgis was born in New York City (1847-1932). In 1869 Sturgis joined a banking firm in New York City and was admitted to membership in the New York Stock Exchange. From 1892-94, he was president of the NYSE during one of the worst stock market panics in history.

Sturgis and his wife were members of Ward McAllister's Four Hundred and spent their summers in Newport. In 1903 Sturgis

---

[216] G. Wayne Miller, "Eileen Gillespie Slocum 1915-2008-Newport's Grande Dame," *The Providence Journal* (29 July 2008), https://www.providencejournal.com/

hired Ogden Codman to build a Tudor style summer home for them on Faxon Green that abutted Cliff Walk.

Sturgis was quite a sportsman and one time president of the Newport Casino. He was also a director of the Redwood Library and president of the Newport Historical Society. He bred horses and was president of the National Horse Shows Association from 1891-1912. In addition, he was a member of the New York Coaching Club and president of the New York Chapter of the ASPCA.[217]

William R. Travers

map WT

Travers (1819-1887) was born in Baltimore and educated at West

Point and Columbia College in New York. He carried on trade in both Baltimore and New York as a commission merchant. About 1853 when business was not good, Travers went to New York to connect with a stock brokerage firm. He partnered with Leonard Jerome, and both made their fortunes on Wall Street.[218]

William Travers was a well-known clubman, belonging to almost 30 social clubs in New York. He entertained by telling stories and was known to have a slight stutter that people found charming. He was a founding member of and large donor to the New York Racquet Club.[219]

Travers had a great deal of input on the founding of Saratoga Racetrack, and he supplied the money for the Travers Stakes.[220]

The Travers family spent most of their summers in Newport in a large estate at the corner of Narragansett and Ochre Point Avenues,

---

[217] "Frank K. Sturgis, Stock Broker, Dies," New *York Times* (16 June 1932), 21.

[218] "America's Successful Men of Affairs," *An Encyclopedia of Contemporaneous Biography*. Ed. Henry Hall (New York: New York Tribune, 1895), I, 665.

[219] Ibid.

[220] Timothy J. Thompson, *Grit and Valor: The Story of Swale* (Bloomington, Indiana: Author House, 2007), 55.

now the site of Salve Regina's Miley Hall.[221] Although Travers did not have the mansion built, he did have Richard Morris Hunt enlarge the house in 1872. He also had Hunt design and build the Travers Block on Bellevue Avenue that runs from Talbot's to the Newport Casino Block.[222]

He and his wife, Maria Louisa Johnson, had nine children. Six of those children and one granddaughter are buried in the family plot.

Travers family burial lot

[221] Baker, 540-541.
[222] Miller, 85.

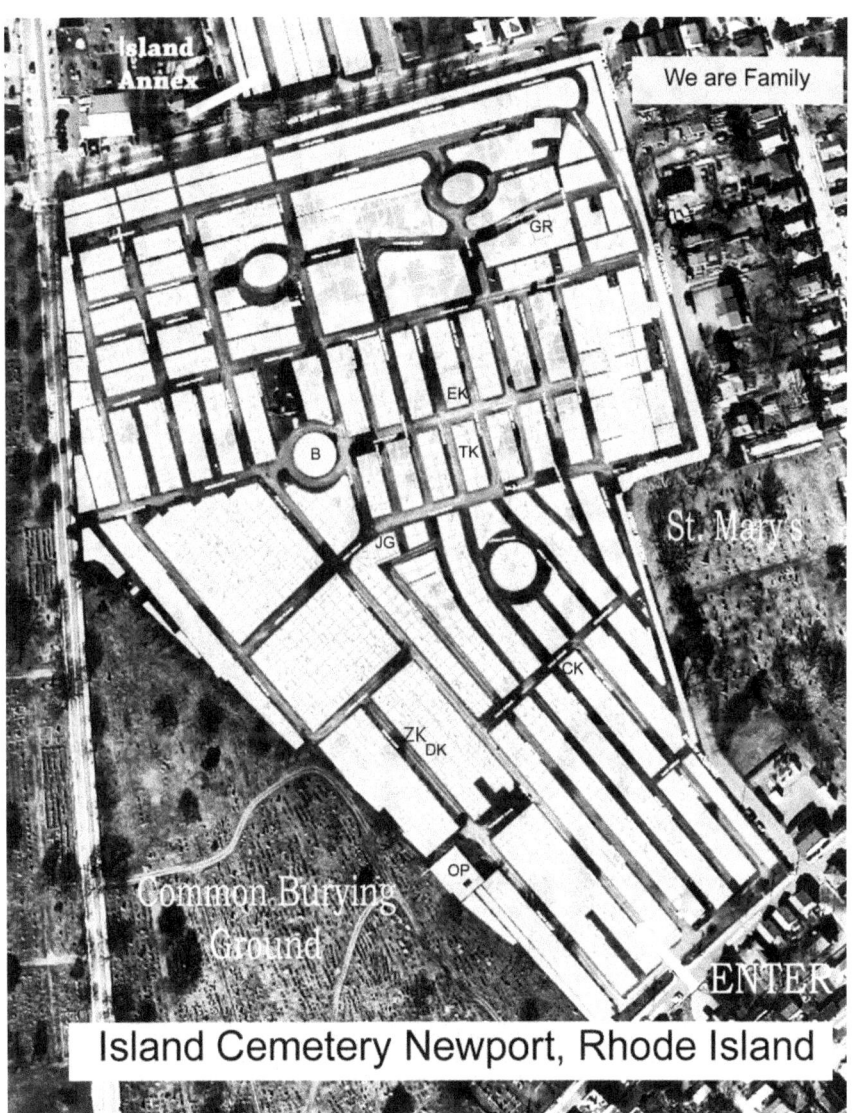

Island Cemetery Newport, Rhode Island

CHAPTER 8

We Are Family

M any families are buried in Island Cemetery and have stories worth sharing. The families selected to be included in this tour may have remarkable stories, may have been prominent in Newport, and/or may have had multiple branches that married into other notable families. There will certainly be more family stories worthy of sharing in the future.

The Perry family

Edmund Perry was the first member of the family to arrive in America in 1630 from Devonshire, England. He was an educated Quaker who spoke publicly about his beliefs, which led to his departure from England to Plymouth, Massachusetts. There he found equal opposition to his beliefs which prompted him to move to South Kingston, Rhode Island

His great-grandson, Freeman Perry (1732-1813), married Mercy Hazard, the daughter of Oliver Hazard, in 1756. Freeman was educated in the law and served in the Colonial Assembly and as judge of the Court of the Common Pleas. Freeman and Mercy were the last members of the Perry family to be members of the Society of Friends.[223]

Captain Christopher Raymond Perry

map B

Captain Christopher Perry
1761-1818

The couple's third son, Christopher Raymond Perry (1761-1818), was born December 4, 1761 in Kingston, Rhode Island. He served during the American Revolution both on sea and on land in a corps known as the Kingston Reds. While serving on a ship as a privateer, he was captured during battle and imprisoned for three months on the Jersey, a prison ship anchored in New York Harbor. After escaping the Jersey, he continued to serve on ships and was later captured and imprisoned for 18 months in Ireland. He was able to escape and make his way back to the Colonies.

After the war, Christopher Perry earned his living on the sea. He was returning from a voyage to Ireland when he met Sarah Alexander (1768-1830), an Irish-born Scottish woman enroute to Philadelphia. A year later (1784) the couple was married in Philadelphia before settling in South Kingston, RI. The Perry estate in South Kingston covered about 200 acres that included a family burial ground.[224]

Their first child, Oliver Hazard Perry, was born August 23, 1785.[225] Other children followed: Raymond Henry Jones Perry (1789-1826), Sarah Wallace Perry (1791-1851), Matthew Calbraith Perry (1794-1858), Anna Maria Perry Rogers (1785-1858), Jane Tweedy Perry Butler

---

[223] Alexander Slidell Mackenzie, *Commodore Oliver Hazard Perry: Famous American Naval Hero, Victor of the Battle of Lake Erie-His Life and Achievements,* (New York: The Werner Company, 1910), 3.

[224] Mackenzie, 6

[225] David Curtis Skaggs, *Oliver Hazard Perry,* (Annapolis, Maryland: Naval Institute Press, 2006), 4.

(1799-1875), James Alexander Perry (1801-1822), and Nathaniel Hazard Perry (1802-1832).

The family moved to 37 Walnut Street in Newport in 1794, about the time of Matthew's birth, and this was their home for the remainder of their lives. Christopher and Sarah Perry were originally buried in the family burial plot in Kingston.

Commodore Matthew C. Perry

map B

Matthew Calbraith Perry (1794-1858) was born in Newport, Rhode Island. His father, Christopher Raymond Perry, and four brothers were active in the early United States Navy. Matthew Perry grew up in Newport, where the family were members of Trinity Church.[226] Perry entered the Navy in 1809, and in 1814 while stationed in New York, married Jane Slidell, daughter of John Slidell, a prominent banker and merchant.[227] Their children were:

- Jane Slidell Perry (c. 1817–1880)
- Sarah Perry (1818–1905), who married Col. Robert Smith Rodgers (1809–1891)
- Jane Hazard Perry (1819–1881), who married Frederic de Peyster (1796–1882) and then John Hone (1819–1891)
- Matthew Calbraith Perry (1821–1873), a captain in the United States Navy and veteran of the Mexican-American War and the Civil War
- Susan Murgatroyde Perry (c. 1825–1896)
- Oliver Hazard Perry (c. 1825–1870)
- William Frederick Perry (1828–1884), 2nd Lieutenant, United States Marine Corps, 1847–1848.

---

[226] John H. Schroeder, *Matthew Calbraith Perry: Antebellum Sailor and Diplomat*, (Annapolis, Maryland: Naval Institute Press, 2001), 6.

[227] Schroeder, 18.

- Caroline Slidell Perry Belmont (1829–1892), who married financier August Belmont
- Isabella Bolton Perry (1834–1912), who married George Tiffany
- Anna Rodgers Perry (c. 1838–1839)[228]

During his career, Matthew Perry was stationed off the coast of Africa and was involved in establishing the first settlement of free Blacks in Liberia. He was appointed to the Brooklyn Navy Yard when not assigned overseas. His most distinguished service was the 1852-1854 expedition to Japan that opened trading with that country.[229]

Perry died in New York City and his funeral took place at St. Mark's Church. His body was placed in the Slidell family vault.

Two of Matthew Perry's daughters played an important role in the final resting place of Perry family members. Caroline Slidell Perry was a delicate beauty known to her family as "Tiny."[230] She met August Belmont in 1849, and the couple married that fall. Her sister, Isabella Bolton Perry, married George T. Tiffany on August 17th 1864. In 1865 Island Cemetery sold a large circular burial plot to August Belmont and George Tiffany, but it is likely the two Perry sisters were the force behind the purchase of the burial plot. In 1865 George Tiffany also purchased the Perry land in South Kingston, Rhode Island.[231] Probably at that time the remains of the Perry sisters' grandparents, Christopher Raymond and Sarah Perry, were relocated to Island Cemetery. Matthew Perry's remains were moved from New York to Island Cemetery in 1866.

---

[228] *Wikipedia*, "Matthew C. Perry," https://en.wikipedia.org/wiki/Matthew_C._Perry

[229] "Death of Commodore M.C. Perry", *New York Times* (5 March 1858), 4.

[230] Schroeder, 155.

[231] National Register of Historic Places Nomination form, 3.

The Belmont family

Map B
August Belmont

Belmont (1813-1890) immigrated to the United Sates from Germany in 1837. He was the representative of the Rothschild Banking

family in America and earned his fortune in New York City. Well-dressed, well-mannered and a devoted family man, Belmont married Caroline Slidell Perry in 1849 and his ties to Newport were established. Belmont was involved in politics and served as chair of the Democratic Party for many years. He was interested in thoroughbred horse racing and is the namesake for the Belmont Stakes, the oldest leg of the Triple Crown. Belmont had the chapel in Island Cemetery built in memory of his daughter Jane Pauline Belmont and gifted it to the cemetery for use by the public.

The Belmont children were:

- Perry Belmont (1851-1947)
- August Belmont, Jr. (1853-1924)
- Fredericka Belmont Howland (1854-1900)
- Jane Pauline (Jennie) Belmont (1856-1875)
- Oliver Hazard Perry Belmont (1858-1908)
- Raymond Rogers Belmont (1863-1887)

Perry Belmont

Perry Belmont
1851-1947

Belmont (1851-1947) was born in New York, later educated at Harvard, the University of Berlin and Columbia Law School. Belmont served as a U.S. Congressman from New York (1880-1888) and the U.S. minister to Spain (1889). He created a social stir when in 1889 he married Jessie Robbins Sloane who had been divorced just a few hours before the nuptials were exchanged. Belmont inherited, owned, but never lived in Belcourt. He died in Newport Hospital at the age of 97. In 1937 he was instrumental in obtaining the Rochambeau statue for the City of Newport. [232]

August Belmont, Jr.

August Belmont (1853-1924) was born in New York to August Belmont Sr. and Caroline Slidell Perry. He was educated at Exeter Academy and Harvard College. In 1875, after graduating from college, he joined his father in business. He was known for his work in finance and horse racing. He organized and financed the New York Subway and the construction of the Cape Cod Canal.

He married twice, first to Elizabeth (Bessie) Hamilton Morgan (in 1881). The couple had three sons, August, Raymond and Morgan. Elizabeth died in 1898. and Belmont married Eleanor Robson in 1910.

Belmont was considered the greatest private breeder of thoroughbred race horses in America. [233]

---

[232] "Perry Belmont, 96, Ex-Diplomat, Dead," *New York Times* (26 May 1947), 1.

[233] "August Belmont, Stricken in Office, Dies in 36 Hours," *New York Times* (11 December 1924), 1.

Fredericka Belmont Howland

Fredricka Belmont (1854-1902) was born in Holland, grew up, and married Samuel S. Howland (1848-1925) in 1877 at Trinity Church in Newport.[234] Howland was the son of Gardiner Greene Howland, one of the founders of the China trade company of Howland and Aspinwall.[235] The other founder of the company, Samuel Shaw Howland, brother of Gardiner, had two daughters that mar-  ried well with Newport connections. Caroline Howland married Charles Handy Russell, a merchant from Providence, and Catherine Clinton Howland married Richard Morris Hunt, architect.

Records indicate she is buried in Greenwood Cemetery in New York. The marker here (with an incorrect death year) may have been erected by a family member in her memory.

Jane Pauline (Jennie) Belmont

Jane Belmont (1856-1875) was a much-loved member of the Belmont family and had been ill for a good part of her life. Her 19 years of life were memorialized in the form of the chapel her family gifted to the Island Cemetery for use by the public.

Raymond Rogers Belmont (1863-1887)

Raymond (1863-1887), son of August and Caroline Belmont, accidently shot himself in the basement of his family home in New York.

---

[234] Black, 519-521.
[235] "Gardiner Greene Howland," *Wikipedia*, https://en.wikipedia.org/wiki/Gardiner_Greene_Howland.

Oliver Hazard Perry Belmont

O.H.P. Belmont (1858-1908) is not buried in Island Cemetery with his family, but his life connects the Belmont family to the Rives family in Newport.

As a young man, Oliver Hazard Perry Belmont lacked the motivation to make a success out of himself. He was named after his famous un-

cle, and his parents, August and Caroline Perry Belmont, hoped he would be as successful in the Navy as his uncle had been. Unfortunately, OHP Belmont found life at Annapolis confining and wanted out. On one of his breaks from school, he met Sara Swan Whiting, who debuted in New York society in 1880, and became infatuated with her. He begged his parents to allow him to leave the Naval Academy and

marry Whiting, but his parents thought both of them were too immature. August Belmont set up a two-year apprenticeship for his son with the Rothschilds Bank and told him if he still felt the same way after the two years were up, he could marry Whiting.[236]

On his way to his apprenticeship in Bremen, OHP Belmont stopped in Paris where he met Whiting and her family. He proposed marriage and she accepted. August Belmont Jr. visited his brother in Paris and tried to talk him out of it but to no avail. He wrote a letter to his parents to advise them that they should allow the marriage to go ahead or be faced with more serious problems. They reluctantly consented.[237]

---

[236] Black, 597-599.
[237] Black, 631-637.

OHP Belmont and Sara Whiting wed on December 27th, 1882 at Swanhurst, her parents' Bellevue Avenue home in Newport, with a number of Mrs. Astor's 400 in attendance. The couple sailed for a two-year honeymoon in January, and Sara's mother and two sisters accompanied them.[238] A few days into their stay in Paris, OHP Belmont asked his bride if they could have their own apartment rather than continue to live with members of her family. When she refused, he left and stayed away for six weeks. During that time Sara discovered

she was pregnant, but by the time Oliver returned, she and her family had sailed for home. He followed, hoping to patch things up, but Sara had already made up her mind that she wanted a divorce.[239]

At the beginning of September 1883, Sara Whiting Belmont gave birth to a daughter she named Natica. OHP Belmont was stopped from seeing his daughter, and for the rest of her life, he denied that Natica was his daughter. Sara Belmont raised Natica on her own but had lots of moral support from New York and Newport society women including Caroline Astor.[240]

Sara obtained her divorce from OHP Belmont in 1885 and four years later married George Lockhart Rives, whom she had known all

---

[238] Wedded at Newport," *New York Times* (28 December 1882), 5.
[239] Black, 659-660.
[240] Black, 662.

her life. Rives wanted to raise Natica as his own, so he adopted her and gave her the surname Rives.[241]

Natica Caroline Rives matured into a popular young lady and was often the subject of newspaper articles in both New York and Newport in part because she was often in the company of an Astor or a Vanderbilt, and the fact that she was Oliver Belmont's daughter was commonly known. She and her parents were part of Mrs. Astor's 400, and newspapers around the country fed the average citizen's curiosity with stories of this young debutante's activities, fashion, and friends.[242]

Natica's closest friend was Cynthia Roche, whose family owned the Elm Court estate on Bellevue Avenue. Roche began seeing Arthur S. Burden, whose family owned the Burden Iron Works in Troy, New York. Burden's brother Williams often accompanied him when he called on Roche, and soon Williams Burden and Natica Rives were seeing each other. After Cynthia Roche and Arthur Burden married in 1906, Natica felt increasing pressure to marry Williams Burden and became ill. He visited her many times to press his suit, and finally Mrs. Rives consented to the marriage. The ceremony at the Rives mansion was small and the couple left for their honeymoon in July of 1907.[243] When they returned six months later, they moved into Burden's mother's home on Fifth Avenue in New York. On February 22, 1908, Natica was found dead in her bedroom. She had apparently been reading by the light of a gas lamp which malfunctioned during the night and she was asphyxiated. The incident was

[241] Black, 664; "A Social Sensation," *The Critic* (18 March 1884), 4; "Wedded Very Quietly," *New York Times* (21 March 1889), 8.

[242] "Newport's Social Life Much Too Strenuous," *Reading Times* (29 July 1903), 4.

[243] "New-York Society," *New-York Daily Tribune* (19 March 1905), 8; "Natica Rives Burden Killed by Gas Leak," *New York Times* (22 February 1908), 2; "Miss Rives Weds Williams P. Burden," *New York Times* (18 April 1908), 11.

ruled an accident by the coroner, but the prevailing rumor was that she had committed suicide.

Natica Rives Burden's funeral was attended by many members of New York society including Natica's biological father, OHP Belmont. After the ceremony, her body was taken by train to the Burden family plot in Troy, New York for burial.[244]

The Tiffany family

map B

Isabella Bolton Perry Tiffany

Isabella (1834-1912) was the daughter of Matthew C. and Jane S. Perry. She and her sister, Mrs. August Belmont, were instrumental in the purchase of the burial circle in Island cemetery and the relocation of their grandparents remains to the site.

George Tiffany

George Tiffany (1805-1886) was a Baltimore merchant who married Isabella Perry. The couple lived at Gravel Court located on Narragansett Avenue and Clay Street. One of their children, George Jr, died in 1878 when he drowned in the waters near Cliff Walk. George Tiffany was a cousin to Charles Lewis Tiffany, who in 1837 founded the jewelry business in New York, Tiffany and Company. Both were grandsons of Ebenezer Tiffany.[245]

---

[244] "Mrs. W.P. Burden's Funeral," *The Brooklyn Daily Eagle* (24 February 1908), 3.
[245] Nelson Otis Tiffany, *The Tiffanys of America: History and Genealogy*, (self-published, 1901), 78.

William Tiffany

William Tiffany (1868-1898) was the son of George and Isabella Tiffany who died as a result of his effort in the Spanish-American War. (For information about his military service, go to the military tour)

Perry Tiffany

Perry (1866-1928), son of George and Isabella Tiffany, was born in Newport and married a daughter of Theodore Havemeyer. He and his second wife, Olive, had relocated to work with the French Red Cross during the war. After the war he went to Dutch Guiana where he had mining interests.[246] He later died in Paris, France.

George Tiffany

George Tiffany (1896-1946) was the son of Belmont Tiffany and grandson of George Tiffany and Isabella Bolton Perry Tiffany. George Tiffany was a student at Harvard when WWI was declared. He enlisted, trained as a pilot and was one of the first American flyers to reach France. He was shot down and held in a German prison camp before escaping. He also served during WWII and achieved the rank of lt. colonel.[247]

Commodore Oliver Hazard Perry

map OP

Oliver Hazard Perry (1785-1819) was born and raised in South Kingston, Rhode Island, the son of Christopher Raymond Perry and older brother of Matthew Calbraith Perry. In his early years Oliver Perry had a gentle manner and a disregard for danger.[248] His education began

---

[246] "Perry Tiffany Dead," *New York Times* (1 July 1928), 25.

[247] "George Tiffany, 50, Found Dead in Bed," *New York Times* (29 November 1946), 25.

[248] Mackenzie, 8.

locally and continued when the family relocated to Newport. While his parents were traveling, twelve-year-old Oliver was in complete charge of his younger siblings. At the age of 13, he was warranted a midshipman in the United States Navy, and he later served during the Quasi-War with France and the Tripolitan War against the Barbary pirates. In 1809 he received his first command, the schooner Revenge.

Perry's fame resulted from his participation in the War of 1812. Perry directed the construction of a fleet on Lake Erie and engaged and defeated the British in battle.[249]

On May 5, 1811, Perry married Elizabeth Champlin Mason of Newport, Rhode Island and they had five children:

- Brigadier General Christopher Grant Champlin Perry, RIM (April 2, 1812 – April 5, 1854) was commander of the Artillery Company of Newport from 1845-1854. He married Muriel Frances Sergeant of Philadelphia (great-granddaughter of Benjamin Franklin.) Their daughter, Margaret Mason Perry, married the artist John LaFarge. Perry was a doctor.
- Oliver Hazard Perry II (February 23, 1813 – March 4, 1814), died in infancy.
- Lieutenant Oliver Hazard Perry, Jr., USN (February 23, 1815 – August 20, 1878), m. 1) Elizabeth Ann Randolph (1816–1847) (Virginia Randolph family)

---

[249] "Oliver Hazard Perry", Naval History and Heritage Command website, https://www.history.navy.mil/browse-by-topic/people/historical-figures/oliver-hazard-perry.

and m. 2) Mary Ann Moseley. When he died, he was involved with mills in Lowell, Massachusetts. One of his children was Oliver Hazard Perry.

- First Lieutenant Christopher Raymond Perry, USA (June 29, 1816 – October 8, 1848), never married.
- Elizabeth Mason Perry, m., as his 2nd wife, the Reverend Francis Vinton, rector of Trinity Episcopal Church in Newport.[250]

Elizabeth Champlin Mason Perry

map OP

Elizabeth Champlin Mason (1791-1858) was born in Newport to Benjamin Mason and Margaret Champlin Mason. The Champlin family was active in Rhode Island for many generations as merchants and politicians. Elizabeth's brother, George Champlin Mason, was the fa-

ther of the Newport architect who was named for him. The architectural work of the younger Mason defines Newport to this day.

---

[250] *Wikipedia,* "Oliver Hazard Perry," http://en.wikipedia.org/wiki/Oliver H. Perry.

The Rives- King Connection

George Lockhart Rives had a sister, Ella Louisa who married David King, Jr. (1839-1894) in 1874.

The King Family

map DK

The first Dr. David King (1774-1836) in Newport arrived from Massachusetts and his family was the main branch of the King family in Newport. Dr. King's union with Anne Gordon of Plainfield, Connecticut in 1806 produced a family of five that included George Gordon, Ann, David, Jr., Edward and William Henry.

Dr. David King (1812-1882)

map TK

Dr. David King, son of Dr. David King and Ann Gordon King, was born in Newport in 1812. He graduated from Brown in 1831 and received his medical degree from Jefferson Medical School in Philadelphia in 1834. He returned to Newport in 1837, married Sarah Gibbs Wheaton and they had seven children. King was one of the founders of the Rhode Island Medical Society and heavily involved in the formation of the American Medical Society.

In addition to his medical practice, King served Newport as a vestryman at Trinity Church, president of the Redwood Library from 1849-1859, and the president of the Island Cemetery Company from 1848-1882.[251]

---

[251] "Dr. David King, Portraits Record PA 106 (Newport, Rhode Island: Redwood Library and Athenaeum) https://redwoodlibrary.pastperfectonline.com/webobject/6886DAC8-3898-4EB8-B226-511199751293.

Edward King

map EK

Edward King (1815-1875) was the third of four sons born to Dr. David King and Ann Gordon King in Newport. His life is detailed in the Architects and Real Estate Tycoons tour.

(Photo published by Digital Commons Salve Regina, 2010)

The family of Edward King poses on the back porch of their mansion around 1873. Edward King (1815-1875) sits at the center. His wife, Mary Augusta LeRoy King (1829-1905), is at the left. Their children from left to right are Alexander Mercer (1869-1885), Edith Edgar (1864-1891), LeRoy (1857-1895), Mary LeRoy (1862-1904), Edward Augustus (1852-1876), Elizabeth Stuyvesant (1855-1878), and George Gordon (1859-1922).[1] Unless otherwise noted, all photographs are from the collection of the Edward King House, Newport.

William Henry King

map TK

W.H. King (1818-1897) was the youngest son of Dr. David King and Ann Gordon King. After graduating from Brown, William Henry King entered the China Trade to join his brothers Edward at the firm of Russell and Company. Unlike his brother, who returned to Newport in less than 10 years, he remained in the trade in China for close to 15 years. In the early 1860s some of his brother's letters contained warnings about alcohol abuse, and some historians claim that W.H. King may have become addicted to opium while in China. Whatever the case, his behavior became more erratic.

In 1864 William Henry King returned to Newport and purchased Kingscote from the family of George Noble Jones. By 1865, however, he was a merchant in Syracuse, New York, and in 1866, his brothers traveled to Troy, New York to stop him from marrying a woman they thought was a fortune hunter. They subsequently had him committed to the McLean Asylum in Boston. He spent the remainder of his life in asylums, suffering from paranoid delusions.[252]

David King Jr.

map TK

David King Jr (1839-1894) was born in Newport to Dr. David King and his wife, Sara Gibbs Wheaton King. He was the first David King in the family to choose something other than the medical profession. Instead, he heeded the advice of his two uncles, Edward and William Henry King, and entered the China Trade at the age of 19.

By the following year, he was working for Russell and Company and earning a handsome salary. In 1870 he married Helen Van

---

[252] King Family Papers, William L. Clements Library, The University of Michigan; Holly Collins, "Kingscote's Coming of Age: A Sentimental Journey," (Newport, Rhode Island: Preservation Society of Newport County, February 24, 2003) 1-5, 22,27.

Cortlandt Morris, but she died a year later from dysentery while pregnant with their child.

David King returned to the United States in 1873 and a year later, married Ella Louise Rives, the sister of George Lockhart Rives. The couple had two children, Philip and Maud Gwendolyn. Like other high society couples, they spent the winter seasons in New York City and the summers in Newport at Kingscote (pictured below), which belonged to David's uncle. While in Newport, King was active as a Trustee for Newport Hospital and a member of the Redwood Library, Newport Reading Room, Newport Casino, and the Redwood Library.

Later in their marriage, the couple spent their winters in Washington, D.C. due to David King's intermittent political appointments. He died suddenly in 1894 at the age of 55 from peritonitis after a case of appendicitis.[253]

---

[253] Ibid.

Theodore Wheaton King

map TK

Theodore Wheaton King was the son of Dr. David King and Sara Gibbs Wheaton King. He died while serving in the Civil War.[254]

Clarence King

map CK

Clarence King (1842-1901) was distantly related to the more well-known King family of Newport, sharing a common ancestor many generations before. King's father, James Rivers King, was also prominent in the China Trade.

Zebulon King

Charles Bird King

map ZK

Zebulon King (1750-1790) was uncle to the original Dr. David King, who settled in Newport in 1799. His son, Charles Bird King (pictured here) was a well-known artist.

---

[254] Article from folder 42 of the William Porcher Miles Papers #508, Southern Historical Collection, (The Wilson Library, University of North Carolina at Chapel Hill, https://web.lib.unc.edu/civilwar/index.php/2011/07/29/29-july-1861-2/

The Griswold Family

map JG

John Noble Alsop Griswold was born in New York City in 1822 to a family who built boats for shipping companies before getting into the China Trade in 1835. In 1847 John Griswold moved to China to handle the overseas part of the business, and he is listed as a partner in the firm of Russell and Company from 1848-1851.[255]

When John Griswold returned to New York about 1851, he was a wealthy man and began to invest in railroads and real estate. He also met his future wife, Jane Emmet. In March of 1860, the couple took their wedding vows at St. Mark's in the Bowery and left for an extended honeymoon in Europe.[256]

While they were in Paris, they met with Richard Morris Hunt and asked him to build them a house in Newport, Rhode Island. The Griswold House, now the Newport Art Museum, was Hunt's first commission in Newport. The Griswolds spent summers in Newport, where JNA Griswold used his time investing money in properties in the summer resort.[257]

JNA Griswold House 1864
Richard Morris Hunt architect

Between 1861 and 1870, the couple had five children, two girls and three boys. Minnie Griswold married John Murray Forbes, a

---

[255] John Pfeiffer, "Historian John Pfeiffer Explores Old Maritime Traditions," *Old Lyme Historical Society Bulletin*, 5 (winter 2009) 5, https://www.oldlymehistoricalso-ciety.org; Sibing He, "Russell and Company in Old Shanghai, 1843-1891," (23-24 May 2011) https://www.amstudy.hku.org.

[256] J. Doyle, "Jane Emmet," (29 February 2012) emmetry, https://www.em-metrydevelopment.com/people/janeemmet.

[257] Baker, 128.

former China Trade associate of her father, in 1882.[258] She was just 19 while he was 32. The couple split their time between New York and Morristown, New Jersey. Two of their children are buried here in the Griswold plot.

Florence Griswold was among the Newporters who married Englishmen and were known as "Dollar Princesses." Her husband, Horatio Robert Odo Cross, was not a nobleman but an army surgeon 21 years her senior. They spent the bulk of their lives in England.[259]

The three sons of JNA and Jane Griswold, all buried here in the Griswold family plot, predeceased their parents. Richard Alsop Griswold, born in 1863, died just over a year after he was born.

John Noble Griswold, born in 1865, attended Columbia College and then attended graduate school there majoring in the field of mining. In the 1890s he moved to Colorado Springs where he died in 1895 of pneumonia just shy of his 30th birthday.[260]

The Griswold's youngest son, Addis Evers Griswold, distinguished himself in both academics and the arts while attending Harvard. He studied for a while in England but returned to attend law school. In 1900 he graduated with his law degree and passed the bar in New York. He practiced law for two years and then had a nervous breakdown.[261]

Jane Griswold had always blamed her husband for pushing their sons too hard, and the couple separated about 1892. She believed her husband was responsible for the premature death of their son John in 1895 and for Addis's nervous breakdown in 1902. She moved Addis to a friend's estate in Pelham, New York and placed him under the care of nurses. On December 23rd, Addis pretended to go to

[258] "Four Weddings Yesterday," *New York Times* (17 February 1882), 6.

[259] "Wed a Grenadier Guard: The Griswold-Cross Nuptials at Newport," *New York Times* (1 May 1892), 8.

[260] *Annual Register of the Officers and Students of Columbia College* (New York: McGowan & Slipper, 1884) 26; "The Summer School, *"Colorado Springs Gazette* (23 July 1895), 5.

[261] "George Griswold's Death," *New York Times* (24 December 1902), 1.

sleep and after the nurse dozed off, he ran to the nearby railroad track where he was struck and killed.[262]

Jane Griswold made a life for herself separate from her husband and joined an artists' colony in the Catskills. While there, she wrote a book called *The Lost Wedding Ring*, featuring a Mrs. Boy, whose story was exactly like that of Jane Griswold. Mrs. Boy, like Jane Griswold, "...decided against taking her divorce, although amply justified...by thus bringing scandal" on the family. The modern woman, according to the novel's protagonist, could stand on her own feet and not obey her husband as they promised in their marriage vows.[263]

While Jane Griswold lived her life in New York pursuing her own interests, JNA Griswold spent his time in Newport. In January 1909, Mrs. Griswold died in at her home in New York. JNA Griswold died 8 months later at his home on Bellevue Avenue.[264] Although the couple had not lived together for nearly 20 years, they were buried side by side in the Griswold plot in Island Cemetery. Both pedestals were originally topped with crosses that have been lost over the years.

---

[262] Ibid.

[263] Candace Wheeler, *Yesterdays in a Busy Life* (New York: Harper and Bros., 1918), 268.

[264] "Died," *New York Times* (22 January 1909), 7; "John N.A. Griswold Dead," *New York Times* (14 September 1909), 20.

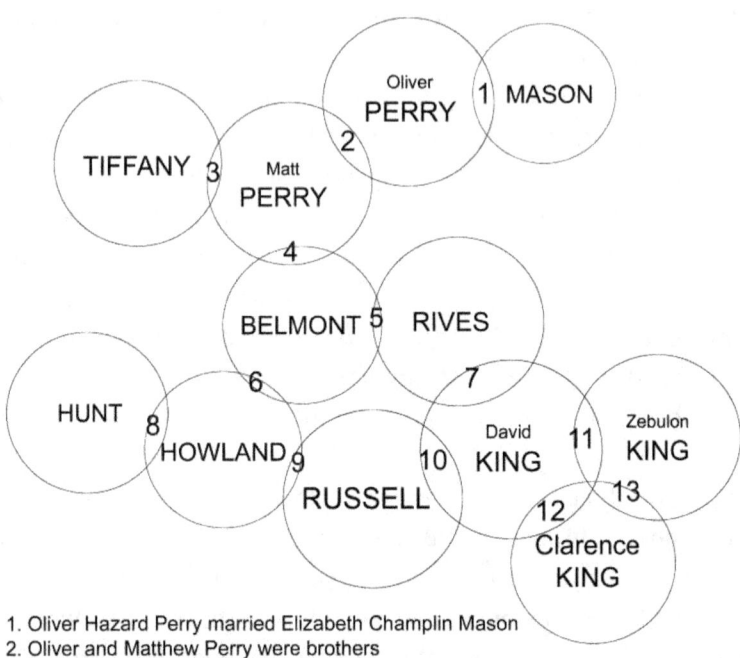

1. Oliver Hazard Perry married Elizabeth Champlin Mason
2. Oliver and Matthew Perry were brothers
3. M. Perry's daughter, Isabella married George Tiffany
4. M. Perry's daughter married August Belmont
5. Sara Swan Whiting married OHP Belmont and later George L. Rives
6. Frederika Belmont married Samuel S. Howland
7. David King, Jr. married Ella Louise Rives
8. Catherine Howland married Richard Morris Hunt
9. Caroline Howland married Charles Handy Russell
10. Charles Howland Russell married Ethel King
11. The father of Zebulon King was the brother of the father of David King
12. Relatives of Clarence King were in the China trade and related to David King
13. Zebulon and Clarence shared relatives

This diagram shows how the families are related.

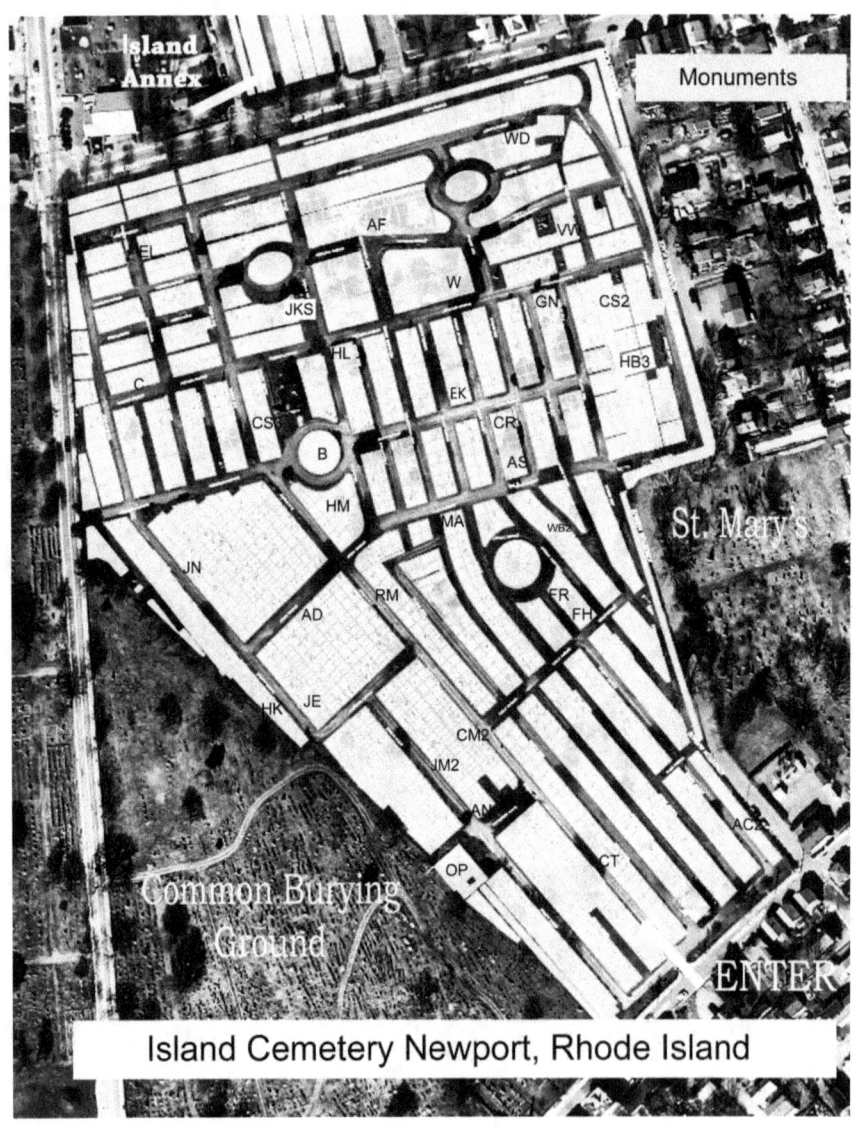

Island Cemetery Newport, Rhode Island

CHAPTER 9

Remarkable Monuments

S electing monuments that are "remarkable" is purely subjective. Those included in this section have features that make them unique in Island Cemetery based on design, material, or designer. Architects of the day are known to have designed grave stones and monuments for wealthier clients. Island Cemetery is fortunate to have such markers created by Richard Morris Hunt, Stanford White and George Champlin Mason, Jr. In addition, artist John LaFarge, Augustus Saint-Gaudens, and Karl Bitter created some of the monuments.

Mausoleums

Island Cemetery boasts at least three noteworthy mausoleums. The first, chronologically, is that of Henry Gurdon Marquand (**map HM**), designed by Richard Morris Hunt in 1885. According to the records at Island Cemetery, the granite mausoleum is designed in the form of a classical temple, and appears to be in the Greek style.

Marquand was a stockbroker, philanthropist and an art collector. He was one of the founders of the Metropolitan Museum of Art and served as its president from 1889 until his death in 1902.

Another interesting mausoleum is that of J.K. Sullivan (**map JKS**). Island Cemetery has no specific information about who designed or built this mausoleum, but it is made of two rough types of stone—one light in color and the other brown. It is the same type of stone

used in the Sullivan Building on Bellevue Avenue, for which J.K. Sullivan was the contractor, so he may have been responsible for the design and building of his own family mausoleum. The exact date this mausoleum was installed is not known, but it was definitely prior to Sullivan's death in 1939.[265]

One of the grandest structures in Island Cemetery is the granite mausoleum constructed for E. Hayward Ferry and his wife, Amelia Parsons Ferry (**map AF**). The designer is unknown, but the style is definitely Art Deco. Ebenezer Ferry was a prominent New York businessman, who was the vice-president of Hanover Bank in New York for nearly two decades. While in Newport, the Ferrys lived at Edgehill, an estate close to that of Mrs. Ferry's sister, Mrs. Arthur Curtiss James.

---

[265] "Jeremiah K. Sullivan Died Wednesday; Prominent Citizen for Over Half Century was 82," *Newport Mercury and Weekly News* (10 March 1939),1.

August Belmont (1816-1890)

map B

This impressive monument was designed by architect Richard Morris Hunt in 1890 and completed in May of 1892 (according to cemetery records). The sculpture work was done by Karl Bitter. The monument includes a Greek exedra with a bench surrounding a Roman triumphal arch which encloses a pink marble sarcophagus covered with palm leaves and olive branches. The arch is supported by Ionic columns and features life-size caryatids. Oliver Hazard Perry Belmont, son of August and Caroline Belmont, commissioned the monument from Hunt.

Additional Richard Morris Hunt monuments

Henry Ledyard (1812-1880)

map HL

Richard Morris Hunt was responsible for the design and building of the marker for the Ledyard plot in 1881-82 and for the redesign in 1893. The dark grey granite false sarcophagus was done in the Roman style and elevated on a classical style catafalque. Henry Ledyard was a founder and first president of Newport Hospital.[266]

Charles Handy Russell (1796-1884)

map CR

According to the records of Island Cemetery, Russell's false sarcophagus was designed and built by Richard Morris Hunt in 1863-64. The Roman style monument has scrolled volutes or

capitals, dentils and friezes. The frieze has triglyphs and metopes which enclose rosettes.

Russell was a merchant in both Providence, Rhode Island and New York City as well as a director of two major banks in Providence and three major East Coast railroads. His summer home in Newport was called Oaklawn, and once stood at the corner of Bellevue and Narragansett Avenues.[267]

---

[266] Https://www.islandcemeterynewport.com; Onorato, *AIA Guide to Newport*, 66.

[267] "Obituary of Charles Handy Russell," *New York Times* (22 January 1884), 5.

Wetmore monument

map W

The family monument for the Wetmore plot was designed and built by Richard Morris Hunt in 1873, not long after he completed the redesign of Chateau-Sur-Mer for George Peabody Wetmore.

Island Cemetery records describe this as a classical pediment with Roman fasces, a symbol of a magistrate's power in ancient Rome. Since G.P. Wetmore was a senator and later governor of Rhode Island, the symbols are appropriate. Also included are ribbons indicating victory and a swag of oak leaves for strength.

Stones by George Champlin Mason and Son

A number of monuments in Island Cemetery were designed by the firm of George Champlin Mason and Son. Likely most of these monuments were designed by the younger Mason. They were all executed in white marble.

Lieutenant William Tiffany (1868-1898)

map B

William Tiffany, a summer resident of Newport and nephew to August and Caroline Slidell Perry Belmont, was one of Teddy Roosevelt's Rough Riders who died of fever and exposure after battles in Cuba during the Spanish-American War. His body, accompanied by Theodore Roosevelt and twelve Rough Riders, was returned to Newport for burial with his family in August of 1898.

His marble grave marker was designed by George Champlin Mason Jr. An article in the *New York Times* ex-
plained the symbolism carved into the marker:

> *"The cross for Lieut. Tiffany's grave suggests the life of promise unfinished, as is shown by the molded or cut work begun, but cut short. The emblematic meanings of the laurel [hero] and oak [strength] add much to the artistic finish. On the top part of the cross the inscription is found, and the military marks "I. K." and crossed swords, copied just twice the size of those Lieut. Tiffany wore on his hat in the service, and which was loaned the sculptor, Mr. Kelley, by Mrs. Tiffany, the dead officer's mother. They are surrounded and supported by clouds, and are the gem of the work...On the bottom of the column there is the inscription:*
>
> *I have fought the good fight,*
> *I have finished my course,*
> *I have kept the faith."* [268]

---

[268] "Monuments at Newport, *New York Times* (2 May 1899), 5.

Bessie Morgan Belmont (1862-1898)

map B

Bessie Morgan Belmont was the first wife of August Belmont Jr. She passed away in Paris, where she had gone to regain her health. Her grave marker is made of Rutland marble and is decorated with a wreath "bride roses [beauty and virtue] and double violets" [death too soon] that were sent to the sculptor from the nursery of her husband. On her cross is one word "Devotion," as she was a very devoted wife and mother.[269] This monument was designed by George Champlin Mason, Jr.

Additional stones designed by GC Mason, Jr.

George Champlin Mason, Jr. (1849-1924) began working as an architect with his father in 1867. In 1871 the firm was renamed George Champlin Mason and Son. Mason Jr. designed 5 additional gravestones for the Tiffany and Belmont plot discussed earlier. They include stones for Jane Pauline Belmont, three men named John B. Newton, Abbie and Charles Spooner and Carrie M. Stewart. While the design of each marble stone varies, the overall visual impact of each stone is similar to the other Mason stones. [270]

---

[269] Ibid.

[270] Ron Onorato, "An Architect and His Environment," 29.

Charles Spooner (1883-1881)

map CS2

Carrie Stewart (1887)

map CS3

John Newton (1833)

map JN

John Newton (1884)

map JN

Martha Maria Anderson (1803-1880)

map MA

Martha Maria Anderson, her husband Elbert and other family members are buried under this triangular marble monument. Martha Anderson was a descendant of Abraham Redwood, Ezra Stiles and William Ellery. After she died in 1880, her husband hired George Champlin Mason to design and build this unusual grave marker. It is in the High Victorian Gothic style inspired by the 1872 Albert monument in London and influenced by 13th century Eleanor crosses.[271]

Anna Theresa Downing (1855)

map AD

The sleeping child was a common image used for children's graves in the mid to late 1800s. This marble stone is a good example of Victorian sentiment.

---

[271] Https://www.islandcemeterynewport.com.

Herbert Barnett (1871-1902)

map HB3

This granite monument has a rustic or natural design and features a broken oak branch. The oak symbolizes many things including strength and endurance and the broken branch represents a life cut short.[272] The information on the scroll includes the Masonic square and compass symbol.

William Birckhead (1840-1895)

map WB2

At first glance this monument looks like a house or small church. Due to the design of the top (roof of the building) it is referred to as a hip tomb.[273] There are a few similarly shaped monuments in the Island Cemetery but this one is nicely detailed, in good condition and executed in granite. Dr. Birckhead lived in a Dudley Newton designed home at 20 Catherine Street. His wife, Sarah, was a daughter of Dr. David King.

---

[272] Keister, 62,66.
[273] Keister, 33.

Adeline Caswell (1838-1913)

map AC2

This monument is fashioned from an alternative material to stone.

Referred to as White Bronze, the material is actually zinc. The Monumental Bronze Company, established in Bridgeport, Connecticut, which operated between 1875 and 1912, was a major manufacturer of these monuments. They were produced in a variety of styles and sizes. There are a few installed in Island Cemetery with details as crisp today as the day they were created. Albert Caswell was a pharmacist and worked with his brother in New York City. His brother was a cofounder of the Caswell-Massey Company in 1872 which was started by Dr. Hunter in Newport in 1752.[274]

Chase

map C

This sizable, natural looking stone is comprised of rose quartz that was possibly harvested from somewhere in New England. Rose quartz is known as the crystal of unconditional

---

[274] "Albert Caswell," *Newport Mercury* (26 February 1927),1.

love and joy.[275]   Members of the family buried here (according to cemetery records) include Sarah A (died 1961), Emily (died 1909), George (died 1943) and Milton (died 1958). Milton graduated from Rogers High School, became an engineer and was known for the installation of water and electricity on Prudence Island[276].

William B DeBlois (1850-1896), Mary E DeBlois (1851-1919)
map WD

This rose-colored granite monument features a marble sphere atop a pedestal. There are a few other monuments in the cemetery with similar design but are missing their spheres. The symbol above William DeBlois' name was originally used by the Knights Templar during the Crusades and later adopted by the Freemasons. The phrase "in loc signo vinces" is Latin for "in this sign (the cross), you will conquer."[277]

William DeBlois served in the Civil War and was injured at Bull Run in 1861.[278] His obituary stated that he was a contractor specializing in masonry and a prominent member of St. John's Lodge of the Freemasons.[279]

---

[275] healing -https://www.healthline.com/health/healing-with-rose-quartz#:~:text=Rose%20quartz%20is%20known%20as,and%20is%20used%20for%20 protection.

[276] "Milton H. Chase, Prudence Island Utilities Owner," *Newport Daily News* (24 February 1958), 2.

[277] Https://www.merriam-webster.com/dictionary.

[278] US Civil War Soldier Records and Profiles 1861-1865, *https://www.Ancestry.com*.

[279] "Newport," *Fall River Daily Evening News* (9 March 1896), 5.

John Eldred (1818-1886)

map JE

The most striking feature of this gravestone is the double-headed eagle with a crown above the heads. The symbol appears to be Russian in origin, but the double-headed eagle symbol is actually for the Ancient and Accepted Scottish Rite of Freemasonry. The number 32 inside the triangle represents the 32nd degree of the Scottish Rite. The Latin motto, "Spes mea in Deo est," means "My hope is in God" and is often included with the use of this image.

Hazard

map FH

This unusual granite monument features an octagonal base with the information about members of the Hazard family for whom it was erected. The Latin word "sinceritas" is engraved on one panel and means honesty and integrity. The tall slender column rising from the center of the base terminates in a cross. The Hazard family was one of the founding families of Newport in 1639.

Henry Kneeland (1865-1900)

map HK

This granite monument features a contemplative woman holding a wreath. While this design can be found in other cemeteries, it is one of the few full figures in Island Cemetery. Since the monument was erected by a mother for her son, it may represent a mother's grief.

Mary Lawton (1896) and Ann Smith (1884)

map AS

This life-size bronze, seated winged woman monument, "Angel of Victory" is one of the most noted in Island Cemetery. It was created in

1897 by Oscar Lenz (1873-1912) who studied under Augustus Saint-Gaudens. Lenz was a graduate of the Rhode Island School of Design and the Ecole des Beaux-Arts.[280] Lawton was the daughter of real estate mogul Alfred Smith and his wife, Ann.

---

[280] Https://www.clarendonvthistory.org/HSWF_DisplayItem?ID=2133&XS=A.

According to cemetery records, the Ann Smith monument was designed by Stanford White and carved by Augustus and Louis Saint-Gaudens. The subject is "Amor Caritas" or Angel of Charity and was based on an 1880 figure for the tomb of Edwin Morgan.[281]

Saint Gaudens in Paris 1898

---

[281]Https://www.nh.gov/nharts/newsandcalendar/spotlights/2022/february.html.

Edward Lawton

map EL

America as a new nation was searching for its identity and turned to ancient democracies for inspiration, such as the Egyptian civilization. Ancient Egyptians were obsessed with providing special care for their deceased and took elaborate steps to send them into the after-life. That was one of the many reasons Americans chose Egyptian themes for their cemetery monuments.[282] The Egyptian Revival movement in architecture and the decorative arts began in the 1880s and continued well into the 1930s.

---

[282] Joy M. Giguere, *Characteristically American*, 3-4.

This monument for four members of the Lawton family includes the winged orb at the top symbolizing the sun god Ra flying across the sky. The symbol was easily adapted into more modern Christian and Jewish beliefs, and the winged orb became a symbol of resurrection. The stylized decoration on the columns includes palm leaves indicating victory over death, inverted chevrons and perhaps lotus flowers used to show rebirth or immortality. [283]

Edward King (1815-1875) and family

map EK

Many King family members are memorialized on this marker that was designed and built 1876-1878. John LaFarge designed the monument and Augustus Saint-Gaudens executed the design in stone. The

subject, "Steps to the Cross" was designated by Mrs. King to recall medieval pilgrimage shrines of Brittany, France. The oak leaves invoke Edward King's favorite tree.[284]

---

[283] Giguere, *Characteristically American*, 68; Keister, 49,63.
[284] Https://www.islandcemeterynewport.com.

Rebecca Thorndike Marin

map RM

This very large granite book is a monument for Rebecca and Mattias Marin. The carving is quite detailed and includes what looks like a shawl or prayer shawl at the bottom. Many people wonder about its meaning, but according to Douglas Keister in his book about gravestone symbolism, a closed book indicates a completed life. [285] The story of the Marin's romance and marriage can be found in the Introductory tour section.

Nearby is an anchor, partially buried in the ground, for Henrietta Marin, one of their daughters. It may be a symbol of her father's naval career or it may stand for hope.[286]

---

[285] Keister, 112.
[286] Keister, 103.

Clara Lewis Moffitt (1859-1884)

map CM2

At first glance this monument may seem as though it marks the grave of a child. Instead, it is a prime example of a Victorian Era grave marker. The dove descending from heaven with a piece of olive branch signifies that the soul has reached divine peace in heaven. The roses signify love and purity, and the hanging flower buds may symbolize sorrow or death at a young age.[287] That fits the deceased, Clara Moffitt, who died at the age of 25.

The back of the stone contains the full name of the deceased and her birth and death dates. The somewhat poetic lines show that the family was a religious one who believed that although they had lost a loved one, they knew that their souls would one day be reunited in heaven.

---

[287] Keister, 43, 54,79.

John Mumford (1796-1821)

map JM2

This gravestone displays many symbols used on stones in the late 1800s. The winged figure represents the soul heading to heaven, and the hourglass indicates that time for life has run out. Laurel, often in wreath form as on this stone, represents eternity as laurel leaves never wilt or fade.

Alexander Nesbitt (1901-1995)

map AN

20th century gravestones were, for the most part, mass produced granite markers that were similar in basic design, shape, and size. This naturalistic granite marker for Alexander Nesbitt, who died in 1995, is unique in its design and setting. Nesbitt was born in 1901 and worked for many years as a graphic designer and teacher. He and his wife Ilse moved to Newport in 1965 and founded the Third and Elm Press. They were some of the early craft people who purchased property in the Point section of Newport, and their efforts led to the resurgence of the neighborhood. This stone is a fitting tribute to Nesbitt.

George Norman (1797-1867)

map GN

The centerpiece of the Norman family burial lot may well be the tallest monument in Island Cemetery.

George Norman made a fortune installing utilities in many places including the water system in Newport.

This large family lot is centered on the 30+ foot fluted column that terminates with a winged toga-clad angel standing on a capital. Additional classic design elements include garlands of flowers.

Table tombs and head and footstones indicate the burial location of the members of the family.

Oliver Hazard Perry (1785-1819)

map OP

Oliver Hazard Perry died while serving the country on a diplomatic mission to Venezuela in 1819. His remains were conveyed to Rhode Island in 1826 and originally interred in the Common Burying Ground. Plans started in 1828 to honor his service to the country with a fitting memorial, and the obelisk that stands today was completed in 1843. Perry's remains were moved to a grave 4 feet south of the monument and marked by two small stones.

The obelisk is 21 ft. 8 inches tall and sits on a mound that is 8 feet high. The stone was deemed unable to receive an inscription so the 5-foot-tall marble pedestal was installed at the base to accommodate the wording noted here:

Oliver Hazard Perry
At the age of twenty-seven,
He achieved
The victory of Lake Erie.

On the north face:
Born in South Kingston, R.I.
August 23, 1785
Died at Port Spain, Trinidad.
August 23, 1819
Aged 34 years

On the west face:
His remains
Were conveyed to his native land
In a Ship of War,
According to a resolution
Of Congress,
And here interred
December 4, 1826

On the south face:
Erected by the State of Rhode Island

Frank Read (1868-1869)

map FR

This monument for the Read family looks quite rustic, but the

rocks show a belief in the power of faith. In the Christian religion, rocks are a symbol of God, and the Old Testament is full of references to rocks.

In Psalms, "The Lord is my rock, and my fortress, and my strength..."

In Matthew, Christ refers to St. Peter as the rock that is the corner-stone of his Church.

In most cultures rocks are a symbol of strength, permanence, and stability.[288]

Charles M. Thurston (1819-1878)

map CT

---

[288] Keister, 123.

According to cemetery records, there are six people buried in this site that resembles a mound of earth that could be called a tumulus. There is no documentation as to why this style of burial was selected, but it is likely the popularity of the side-hill tomb at Mt. Auburn Cemetery[289] inspired Thurston to use this style of tomb. Since the topography of Island Cemetery was flat, a mound was created rather than using the side of a hill. Charles Myrick Thurston (-1844) was a Newport native, successful New York City merchant, an active member of the New Rochelle Historical Society and an avid genealogist.[290]

Vitello-Winkler

map VW

When the Island Cemetery was established, stone bench monuments were installed to allow a place for visitors to sit when visiting a loved one's grave. This 21st century bench monument has its roots in that tradition but is executed in a contemporary design.

---

[289] Joy M. Giguere, "Palaces for the Dead: The Mausoleum Craze in Gilded Age America," Markers XXXVII (Greenfield, Massachusetts: The Association for Gravestone Studies, 2021), 124.

[290] Https://www.gibbesmuseum.org/miniatures/collection/detail/CB2DCBD4-A94F-4290-8D9F-199711448157.

Complete Map and List of Notable Burials and Monuments

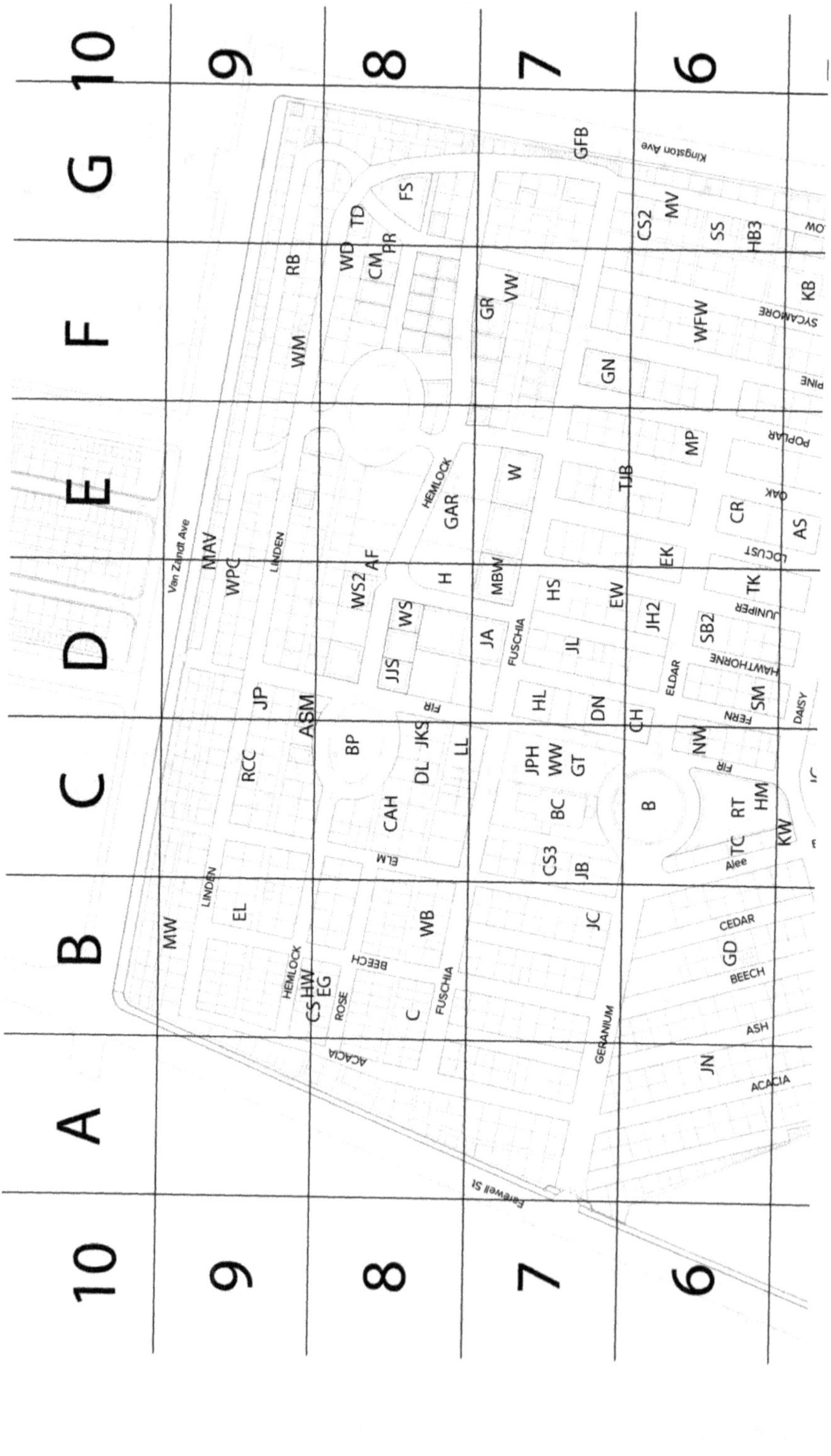

10
9
8
7
6
A
B
C
D
E
F
G
Van Zandt Ave
Kingston Ave
Farewell St
LINDEN
HEMLOCK
FIR
ELM
BEECH
ROSE
FUSCHIA
ACACIA
GERANIUM
CEDAR
ASH
SYCAMORE
PINE
POPLAR
OAK
LOCUST
JUNIPER
HAWTHORNE
ELDAR
FERN
DAISY
Alee
MW
EL
CS
HW
EG
C
WB
RCC
JP
ASM
BP
CAH
DL
JKS
LL
JPH
WW
GT
BC
CS3
JB
JC
B
RT
HM
TC
KW
NW
CH
GD
JN
MAV
WPC
WS2
AF
WS
JJS
H
JA
MBW
HS
JL
HL
DN
EW
JH2
SB2
SM
TK
EK
GAR
W
TJB
CR
AS
MP
WM
RB
WD
CM
PR
TD
FS
GR
VW
GN
WFW
KB
GFB
CS2
MV
SS
HB3

Notable graves in Island Cemetery

A B C D E F G

1 2 3 4 5

Streets: WILLOW, SYCAMORE, PINE, ROSE, POPLAR, OAK, LOCUST, JUNIPER, HAWTHORNE, MAGNOLIA, FERN, CEDAR, BEECH, ELM, DAISY, ASH, ACACIA, CLEMATIS, MONUMENT PLACE, HAWTHORNE, Werner St, Alee

Grave markers: HB3, KB, GB, MS, AS, RF, SF, GW, WB2, AC, FR, FH, WT, SP, LG, MA, DF, CE, DK2, CV, HT, CK, JF, SB, LOCUST, JAH, OF, AC2, GG, WG, CT, AM, HC, JG, GC, RM, BT, GM, TS, JPP, CM2, JM2, DK, ZK, AN, EA, MM, HB, WJS, EB, VS, OP, WC, IG, JH, ASH, JM, CGM, AD, JP, KW, HM, SM, TK, GT, DAISY, JW, MC, HK, AKM, JE, HB2, CB, HBS, KB

Island Cemetery Notable Burials

map symbol	grid location	First name	Last name	Born-died	comment
OF	E1		CEMETERY OFFICE		1901-1902 designed by Herbert Wilson
EA	C2	Egypt Air/vault			monument to those who died in Egypt Air Flight 990; site of a 1902 receiving vault
MA	D5	Martha	Anderson	1803 -1880	Gothic monument
JA	D7	Hugh	Auchincloss	1897-1976	during WWII was in Naval intelligence; married Janet Bouvier in 1942 and became the stepfather of the First Lady of the United States, Jackie Kennedy; supporter of the Boys Club of Newport and a board member of the Redwood Library
JA	D7	Janet	Auchincloss	1907 -1989	mother of Jacqueline Bouvier Kennedy Onassis, wife of President Kennedy
JB	C7	Joe	Bailey	1802-1877	builder and partner with Alfred Smith
HB3	G6	Herbert	Barnett	1871-1902	rustic designed monument featuring broken oak limb symbolizing a life cut short

MBW	D7	Edna	Barger	1872 -1957	lived in and owned Edna Villa, also known as the Isaac Bell House, for longer than any other family (1891-1952)
WB	B8	Lt. Willett Clark	Barrett	1895- 1918	killed in action in France during WWI; received Purple Heart
SB2	D6	Seth	Bateman	1802- 1887	created a summer hostelry that served high society guests from around the world
JH2	D6	Henry	Bedlow	1821 -1914	mayor
B	C6	Eleanor Robson	Belmont	1878- 1979	actress greatly admired by many including G. B. Shaw; founder in 1935 of the NY Metropolitan Opera Guild and a great supporter of the Red Cross.
B	C6	August	Belmont	1813- 1890	banker, horseman; husband of Caroline Slidell Perry; monument designed by RM Hunt
B	C6	Perry	Belmont	1851- 1947	served during the Spanish-American War; US Congressman from NY
B	C6	Bessie Morgan	Belmont	1862- 1898	wife of August Belmont, Jr; monument designed by GC Mason, Jr.
B	C6	August	Belmont Jr	1853- 1924	organized and financed the NYC subway and the Cape Cod Canal

CB	A5	Charles	Bevins	1844-1925	architect for many shingle style Jamestown buildings including Horsehead
WB2	E5	William	Birckhead	1840-1895	hip tomb; married daughter of Dr. David King; lived in a Dudley Newton designed house at 20 Catherine Street
GB	G5	Gladys Carr	Bolhouse	1899-1995	The first official historian of the City of Newport; served as Navy Yeoman F during WWI.
EB	C2	Edith	Bozyan	1908-1993	artist who founded the DeBlois Gallery in 1984
SB	E3	Seth	Bradford	1801-1874	master builder or architect; designed the original Chateau-sur-Mer and other buildings
GFB	G7	Gunner George F. (Patrick)	Brady	1867-1903	Congressional Medal of Honor awarded for efforts at Cuba during Spanish-American War
KB	F5	Capt. Kidder Randolph	Breese	1831-1881	participated in Perry's expedition to Japan in 1854; served during the Civil War; served as Commander of the Newport Torpedo Station
HB2	B4	Brevet Brigadier Henry	Brewerton	1801-1879	entered West Point at age 12; supervised the building of forts; served

					as superintendent of West Point 1845-1852
HB	C2	Melville	Bull	1854-1909	US Representative from RI 1895-1903
HB	C2	Henry	Bull	1815 -1899	involved with creation of Island Cemetery and its 2nd president
TJB	E7	Truman J	Burdick	1839 -1908	mayor of Newport 1879-1880; served in the Civil War; founder of Newport Street Railway; known for charitable work
RB	F9	Robert S	Burlin-game	1864 -1945	served as mayor of Newport and was elected in 1905 to the state legislature and served 3 terms; Deputy Speaker of the House in Rhode Island
GC	C5	George Henry	Calvert	1803-1889	served as Mayor of Newport but also known as a writer; acquainted with Longfellow, Emerson, and Poe. A direct descendant of the founder of Maryland and president of the Perry Monument Association.
MC	B5	Marion	Carry	1905-1987	artist who taught for 5 decades at the Newport Art Association where

					she also assisted Helena Sturtevant.
AC	E4	Rear Admiral Augustus	Case	1813-1893	served in the Mexican-American War and the Civil War
AC2	E1	Adeline	Caswell	1838-1913	white bronze monument
BC	C7	Belmont	Chapel	1886, 1891	chapel designed by G.C. Mason and altered by R.M. Hunt for Belmont family
JC	B7	John Rose	Caswell	1834-1918	Caswell and Massey founder
C	B8		Chase		rose quartz monument
WPC	D9	William P	Clarke	1870-1937	served as mayor of Newport 1907-1909 and RI Legislature 1906; operated Franklin News Depot and helped develop championship high school basketball teams
TC	C6	Thomas	Coggeshall	1829-1900	former mayor and city councilman; school named for him; helped open Wickford to NY train line; involved with laying out Ocean Drive
RCC	C9	Robert C	Cottrell	1853-1932	served as Mayor of Newport in 1905; was an undertaker in the city and vestryman at Trinity Church for 42 years

WC	C1	William Cole	Cozzens	1811-1876	mayor of Newport 1854-55; state representative and senator; bank president
HC	D1	William	Cranston	1821-1871	mayor of Newport 1857-1866;
HC	D1	Henry	Cranston	1789-1864	US representative from RI 1843-1847; 3 years served as speaker of the RI House
HC	D1	Robert B	Cranston	1791-1873	US Representative from RI 1837-1843; served in RI State Senate and House; declined office of mayor when elected
TD	G8	Theodore Montgomery	Davis	1837-1915	Egyptologist and owner of "The Reefs", now Brenton State Park
WD	F8	William	DeBlois	1850-1896	granite sphere monument
AD	B5	Anna Theresa	Downing	1853c-1855	sleeping child monument
GD	B6	George T	Downing	1819-1903	leading Civil Rights leader in the nation.
TE	E10	Lt. Thomas	Eadie	1887-1974	Medal of Honor awarded for rescuing a fellow diver in 1927
JE	B4	John	Eldred	1818-1886	Scottish Rites eagles on monument
DF	D5	Daniel	Fearing	1859-1918	served the city in many ways including as president of the Newport Historical Society.
CE	D5	Christopher	Ellery	1768-1840	US Senator from RI

AF	E8	Amelia	Ferry	1865 -1945	Art Deco style tomb
JF	E3	James C	Fludder	1847-1901	architect, builder, stone mason; studied with G.C. Mason; designed schools and firehouses
RF	E4	Robert	Franklin	1836-1913	Newport mayor 1882-1885; served on Newport City Council for 10 years, 6 years as president; bakery at the corner of Spring and Mary Streets
SF	E4	Susan B.	Franklin	1868-1955	teacher and historian who contributed many articles to the Newport Historical Society.
LG	D4	Levi H	Gale	1793-1853	in 1853 had Russell Warren design and build a home for him on Washington Square. In 1925 the house was cut in half and relocated uphill to serve the Jewish Congregation.
GAR	E8		GAR		The Grand Army of the Republic was a nationwide organization serving veterans of the Civil War.
HW	B8	Evanda	Garnett	1896-1918	Royal flyer who died while serving in WWI
IG	C1	Isaac	Gould	1783-1853	Tailor who trained Alfred Smith (later real estate tycoon). His family

					were the caretakers of the synagogue when it was closed 1822-1880s. His son, Nathan, married the daughter of architect Isaiah Rogers.
WG	D1	William Channing	Gibbs	1787-1871	sold land that is Touro Park to the city; was RI Governor 1821-1824, the last under the Charter of 1663
GG	E1	George Washington	Greene	1811-1883	writer and historian
JG	C5	John NA	Griswold	1822-1909	land owner; had R.M. Hunt design house that today is the Newport Art Museum
JG	C5	Jane Emmet	Griswold	1832-1909	writer who opened her Newport home to orphans and meetings of the Town and Country Club.
JH2	D6	J Prescott	Hall	1796-1862	served as US District Attorney for the Southern District of New York; hired Alexander Jackson Davis to build estate on Malbone ruins; monument has Egyptian Revival design
CAH	C8	Charles A	Hambly	1916-2008	Newport Mayor 1961-1965; served as a bombardier in WWII;
CH	CD6	Charles E	Hammett Jr	1823-1902	published George Champlin Mason's *Reminiscences*

JH	B2	Major John	Handy	1756-1828	read the Declaration of Independence to the gathered citizens at the Colony House in Newport on July 20, 1776 and 1826.
JAH	D1	John Alfred	Hazard	1843-1920	owned land, real estate speculator
FH	E4	Francis	Hazard	1885-1975	octagon with pillar monument
JPH	C7	Jane Pickens	Hoving	1907-1992	American actress who appeared in the Ziegfield follies and in films.
H	D8	Richard Morris	Hunt	1827-1895	America's premier architect; designed the Breakers, Marble house and others
H	D8	Richard Howland	Hunt	1862-1931	worked with father; involved with design of the Metropolitan Museum of Art in NYC
DK2	C5	Delancey Astor	Kane	1844-1915	West Point graduate; Newport alderman; started Coaching in America; served as president of the NY Yacht Club
EK	E6	Edward	King	1815-1875	involved in China Trade; had Richard Upjohn design the Edward King House; major land owner in Newport;
DK	C3	George Gordon	King	1807-1870	US Representative 1849-1853

ZK	C3	Charles Bird	King	1785-1862	American artist who specialized in Native American portraits
CK	E3	Clarence	King	1842-1901	founder and director of the US Geological Survey; prominent in Gilded Age NY society but was secretly married to an African American woman
CK	E3	William Vernon	King	1838-1864	officer in an all-Black unit during the Civil War; killed at Petersburg in 1864
ZK	C3	Zebulon	King	1750-1790	served during the American Revolution; moved to Ohio where he was killed by Native Americans and is likely buried; son, Charles Bird King, painted portraits of Native Americans.
DK	C3	Dr. David	King	1774-1836	gave first smallpox vaccine in RI; president of the Redwood Library
EK	E6	Frederick Rhinelander	King	1887-1972	architect of the Seamen's Church Institute in Newport and other buildings
TK	D6	Theodore Wheaton	King	1841-1862	Injured in the Battle of Bull Run on July 21, 1861; died in February 1862 as a result of his wounds.
TK	D6	William Henry	King	1818-1897	earned fortune in the China trade; bought

					property from George Noble Jones later known as Kingscote
TK	D6	David	King, Jr	1839-1894	entered China Trade and earned fortune; later owned Kingscote
HK	A4	Henry	Kneeland	1865-1900	classic female statue monument
JL	D7	John G	Ladd	1807-1890	architect- designed Littlefield house on Pelham Street and other buildings
AS	E5	Mary	Lawton	1858-1896	angel monument designed by Oscar Lenz
EL	B9	Edward	Lawton	1847-1931	Egyptian Revival monument
LL	C8	Lewis Cass	Ledyard	1851-1932	lawyer to prominent men of business and companies; president of the New York Public Library, trustee of the Metropolitan Museum of Art; in Newport active in the Casino and the Reading Room; gifted money to Newport Hospital founded by his father.
HL	D7	Henry	Ledyard	1812-1880	Mayor of Detroit, US Senator from Michigan, founder and first president of Newport Hospital; false sarcophagus designed by RM Hunt

DL	C8	Dean	Lewis	1916-1997	mayor of Newport 1951-1953
AKM	B4	Andrew Kirk	McMahon	1841-1921	Served in the Civil War; superintendent of Island Cemetery 1871-1921; active in Newport community including Emmanuel Church for 35 years
WM	F9	William	MacLeod	1883-1960	youngest elected mayor of Newport at 29 years old; WWI veteran
CM	F8	Charles Howard	Malcom	1832-1899	false sarcophagus
CM	F8	Princess Alexandra Troubetzkoy	Malcom	1910-1994	born a Russian Princess; trained artist
MM	C2	Mark	Malkovich III	1930-2010	director of the Newport Music Festival for 35 years
RM	C5	Rebecca	Marin	1823-1890	book-shaped monument
HM	C6	Henry Gurdon	Marquand	1819-1902	part of the group that established the Metropolitan Museum of Art in NYC; Newport home and tomb designed by RM Hunt; member of Newport Town and Country Club
SM	D6	Samuel	Marsh	1798-1874	Egyptian Revival monument

GM	C4	George Champlin	Mason	1820-1894	artist, publisher, writer, architect; designed more buildings in Newport than any other architect and trained other architects; very involved with Trinity Church
JPH	C7	Marcella	McCor-mack	1930-2010	conservationist; Jane Pickens's daughter
AM	D1	Alexander	McGregor	1796-1870	architect, builder mostly using stone; projects include Fort Adams and the Artillery Company headquarters
CM 2	C3	Clara	Moffitt	1859-1884	open door monument
AS M	CD 9	Amanda S	Muenchin ger	1854-1921	hotels; guest houses
CG M	C4	Charles G.	Muenchin ger	1827-1898	confectioner
AS M	CD 9	Gustave A	Muenchin ger	1854-1915	hotels; guest houses
JM2	C3	John	Mumford	1796-1821	figure with hourglass on monument
JM	C4	Josiah Smith	Munro	1805-1861	Monroe family monuments feature urn, ivy, ferns, rushes, oak leaves
AN	C2	Alexander	Nesbitt	1901-1995	modern monument
JN	A6	John	Newton	1800-1833 1826-1884	monument designed by George Champlin Mason, Jr.

DN	D7	Dudley	Newton	1845-1907	architect trained by G.C. Mason; designed many buildings in Newport
GN	F7	George H	Norman	1827-1900	established the *Newport Daily News* in 1935, and the Newport Waterworks; impressive column with figure monument
BP	C8	Bud	Palmer	1921-2013	basketball player; sportscaster
SP	D4	Samuel A	Parker	1810-1872	mayor of Newport and RI State Treasurer for 15 years
JP	B4	Job Almy	Peckham	1807-1885	1838-1923- operated a lumber yard and was a builder; many houses on Kay Street
JPP	C4	John P	Peckham	1841-1861	killed at Bull Run during the Civil War
MP	E6	Mildred Olive Bigelow	Pell	1886-1980	artist, author and writer of a condensed version of the *King James Bible*
OP	C2	Elizabeth Champlin Mason	Perry	1791-1858	wife of OH Perry; cousin of GC Mason
B	C6	Capt. Christopher Raymond	Perry	1761-1818	served during the American Revolution; father of Oliver H. and Matthew C. Perry
B	C6	Commodore Matthew C.	Perry	1794-1858	U.S. Navy officer opened trade with Japan in 1854; his daughter married August Belmont

OP	C2	Commo-dore Oli-ver H.	Perry	1785-1819	hero of the Battle of Lake Erie during the War of 1812
JP	D9	Lt. Colo-nel John Hare	Powel Jr	1837-1908	served during the Civil War and later as Mayor of Newport and RI Sena-tor; involved in Red-wood Library, Reading Room and Newport Hospital
FR	E4	Frank	Read	1868-1869	rustic designed monu-ment
PR	F8	Philip Mercer	Rhine-lander	1869-1939	Bishop of Pennsylvania 1911-1925
GR	F7	George Lockhart	Rives	1849-1917	US Assistant Secretary of State; active in NYC including Metropolitan Opera House, NY Public Library; in Newport was involved with the New-port Historical Society and the Casino and the formation of the Spout-ing Rock Beach Associa-tion.
GR	F7	Sarah Swan Whiting Belmont	Rives	1861-1924	first wife of OHP Bel-mont and later wife of George Rives
CR	E6	Charles Handy	Russell	1796-1884	merchant; director of banks and railroads; sar-cophagus designed by RM Hunt
VS	C2	Virginia	Sampson	1908-2001	worked 70 years at Is-land Cemetery

WS2	D8	William Paine	Sheffield Jr	1857-1919	Newport Representative to RI multiple times and Rep. to US Congress in 1909-1911
WS	D8	William Paine	Sheffield Sr.	1820-1907	US Representative and Senator
TS	C4	Major General Thomas West	Sherman	1813-1879	appointed to West Point; served during the Mexican-American and Civil Wars
JJS	D8	John Jermain, Jr	Slocum	1941-2017	Director of the Alletta Morris McBean Charitable Trust; director of the Redwood Library and President and CEO of the Preservation Society of Newport County (1989-1999)
JJS	D8	Eileen Gillespie	Slocum	1915-2008	major supporter of the Republican Party and subject of a 2010 film, *Behind the Hedgerow*
SS	G6	Stephen P	Slocum	1818-1902	mayor of Newport 1880-1882
AS	E5	Alfred	Smith	1809-1886	landowner who developed the Kay-Catherine Street development, the mansion area, and Ocean Drive
AS	E5	Anna	Smith	1820-1884	John LaForge designed monument; Alfred Smith's wife
CS	B8	Clarence	Stanhope	1852-1924	photographer of many buildings in Newport; bookkeeper at the

					Newport Casino for four decades
CS2	G6	Charles	Spooner	1833-1881	monument designed by George Champlin Mason Jr.
CS3	C7	Carrie	Stewart	1887	monument designed by George Champlin Mason Jr.
HS	D7	Brevet Brigadier General Hazard	Stevens	1842-1918	twice injured during the Civil War; received the Congressional Medal of Honor
HS	D7	Major General Isaac Ingalls	Stevens	1818-1862	West Point graduate who served in the Mexican-American and Indian Wars; the Governor of Washington Territory; killed during the Battle of Chantilly during the Civil War; son Hazard was wounded in the same battle.
MS	E5	Maude Lyman	Stevens	1869-1949	author, historian, especially about Rhode Island and Newport history; served as director of the Newport Historical Society
FS	G8	Frank K	Sturgis	1847-1932	NYSE president, member of Mrs. Astor's 400, coaching, horse racing; SPCA; Newport Casino, Redwood Library director and president of the Newport Historical

					Society; house in Newport designed by Ogden Codman
JKS	C8	Jeremiah Kirrian	Sullivan	1857-1939	general contractor, street commissioner, banker and director of several Newport companies; his building stands on Bellevue Ave across from the Redwood Library; buried in a fine tomb in the cemetery.
JKS	C8	John J	Sullivan	1896-1973	mayor of Newport 1953-1957
WJS	D2	William J	Swinburne	1823-1897	mayor of Newport 1855-1857; served in the Mexican-American War
RT	C6	Roderick	Terry	1849-1933	president of the Newport Historical Society and the Redwood library; paid for the installation of Rochambeau at King Park and was involved with the restoration of the Colony House and the expansion of the Redwood library
GT	B5	Brevet	Tew	1829-1884	served during the Civil War

		Brigadier General George W			
CT	D1	Charles M	Thurston	1819 -1878	family hillside tomb
B	C6	George	Tiffany	1805- 1886	married Isabella Perry, sister of Mrs. Belmont and daughter of MC Perry; Tiffany had Gravel Court built on Narragansett Ave; shared a grandfather with the founder of the Tiffany jewelry business
B	C6	George	Tiffany	1896- 1946	one of the early WWI flyers; shot down and imprisoned for months; served also in WWII
B	C6	Isabella	Tiffany	1834- 1912	monument designed by George Champlin Mason Jr.
B	C6	William	Tiffany	1868- 1898	served as a Rough Rider with Teddy Roosevelt during the Spanish-American War; died from illness contracted in Cuba; monument created by G.C. Mason Jr.
WW	C7	Gabriel Mead	Tooker	1839- 1905	NY society, the 400, memorial here but buried elsewhere
BT	C5	Commodore Benjamin J	Totten	1806- 1877	served during the Civil War; wrote textbook used to train Naval officers

WT	D4	William R	Travers	1819-1887	NY clubman, founder of the NY Racket Club and a racetrack in Saratoga NY that now hosts the Travers Stakes, the oldest stakes in the US; had RM Hunt design shops that still stand on Bellevue Ave. at Memorial Blvd.
HT	D3	Henry E	Turner	1816-1897	served as doctor to Newporters for 60 years and was involved in the city in many positions; President of the Newport Historical Society and secretary of Willow Cemetery; documented graves in the city
MAV	DE 9	Mathias Alonzo	Van Horne	1871-1932	first African American dentist in the state; founding member of the Newport NAACP, active in fraternal organizations and church
MV	G6	Mahlon	Van Horne	1840-1910	Pastor at Union Congregational Church for 28 years; first person of color elected to the Newport School Committee (1872) and the first person of color elected to the state legislature (1885)
CV	CD 5	Charles C	Van Zandt	1830-1894	34th Governor of RI also served in the State

					House as speaker; improved RI education system
MB W	D7	Maud	Wallach	1870-1954	US Tennis National Champion and longtime resident of the Isaac Bell House with her sister
GW	E4	Major General Gouverneur K	Warren	1830-1882	hero of the Battle of Antietam where his actions defended Little Round Top, an important point in the battlefield
WW	C7	Whitney	Warren	1864-1943	architect - designed the Newport Country Club and Grand Central Station in NYC
JW	B5	John G	Weaver	1812-1892	operated Ocean House Hotel and others
W	E7	George Peabody	Wetmore	1846-1921	family monument designed by RM Hunt; 37th governor of RI 1885-1887; US Senator 1895-1907; involved with construction of RI State House, Lincoln Memorial in Washington DC, Grant Memorial, organizer of Metropolitan Opera; one of the founders of the Jockey Club, Redwood Library trustee, president Newport Hospital and Redwood Library; had RM Hunt renovate home, Chateau-sur-Mer

W	E7	Edith	Wetmore	1870-1966	active in the Cooper-Hewitt Museum in NYC, the Newport Art Association and the Old Statehouse Committee
W	E7	Maud	Wetmore	1873-1951	avid golf and tennis player; active in the National Republican Party and Women's Defense Work during WWI
MW	B9	Marcus	Wheat-land	1868-1934	the first doctor in Newport to use x-rays as a diagnostic tool; served on Newport City Council and was a member of numerous medical organizations.
HW	B9	Henry S	Wheeler	1894-1967	served in the Navy during WWI and as a Marine in WWII; elected Mayor of Newport
WF W	F6	William F	Wilbor	1836-1904	builder Kay-Catherine area including the Calvert-Cranston school
EW	D7	Edwin	Wilbur	1867-1943	architect - designed 1902 vault in Island Cemetery, fire house #5 on Touro Street and the Armory on Thames
NW	C6	Nina Maud	Wilks	1869-1930	20th century slate shows she was a teacher
KW	C5	Katherine Prescott	Wormeley	1830-1908	Civil War nurse; founder of Newport Charity Organization Society; translator of French literature
VW	F7	Vitello	Winkler	1963-2017	modern style bench monument

Selected Bibliography

Not all sources are listed in the bibliography. Check specific footnotes for complete information about a source.

BOOKS AND ARTICLES

Atlas of the City of Newport, Rhode Island. Springfield, Massachusetts: L.J. Richards & Company, 1893.

Atlas of the City of Newport, Rhode Island. Springfield, Massachusetts: L.J. Richards & Company, 1907.

Baker, Paul R. *Richard Morris Hunt*, Cambridge, Massachusetts: The MIT Press, 1980.

Black, David. *The King of Fifth Avenue: The Fortunes of August Belmont.* New York: Dial Press, 1981.

City Atlas of Newport, Rhode Island. Philadelphia, Pennsylvania: G.M. Hopkins, 1876.

Collins, Holly. "Kingscote's Coming of Age: A Sentimental Journey." Newport, Rhode Island: Preservation Society of Newport County, February 24, 2003.

Cothran, James R., and Erica Danylchak. *Grave Landscapes: The Nineteenth Century Cemetery Movement.* Columbia, South Carolina; University of South Carolina Press, 2018.

Farber, Jessie Lee. *Symbolism in the Carvings on Old Gravestones*. Greenfield, Massachusetts: Association for Gravestone Studies, 1986.

Giguere, Joy M. *Characteristically American: Memorial Architecture, National Identity, and the Egyptian Revival*. Knoxville, Tennessee: The University of Tennessee Press, 2014.

Giguere, Joy M. "Palaces for the Dead: The Mausoleum Craze in Gilded Age America," *Markers XXXVII*. Greenfield, Massachusetts: The Association for Grave-stone Studies, 2021.

Journal and Letters of Edward King 1835-1844. Ed. Ethel King Russell. New York: no publisher, 1934.

Kathrins, Michael C. *Newport Villas.* New York: W.W. Norton and Company, Inc., 2009.

Keister, Douglas. *Stories in Stone: A Field Guide to Cemetery Symbolism and Iconography*. Salt Lake City, Utah: Gibbs Smith, Publisher, 2004.

King Family Papers, 1844-1901. Ann Arbor, Michigan: The University of Michigan, 1996.

Mackenzie, Alexander Slidell. *Commodore Oliver Hazard Perry: Famous American Naval Hero, Victor of the Battle of Lake Erie, His life and Achievements*. Akron, Ohio: The Superior Printing Company, 1915.

Miller, Paul. *Lost Newport*. Bedford, Massachusetts: Applewood Books, 2008.

Onorato, Ronald J., and American Institute of Architects. Rhode Island Chapter. *AIA Guide to Newport.* Providence, Rhode Island: American Institute of Architects, Rhode Island Chapter, 2007.

Onorato, Ron. "An Architect and His Environment: The Career of George Champlin Mason Jr." *Newport History: Journal of the Newport Historical Society,* Summer/Fall 2019. Issue 91, no. 280.

Sandweiss, Martha. *Passing Strange.* New York: Penguin Press, 2009.

Schroeder, John H. *Matthew Calbraith Perry: Antebellum Sailor and Diplomat.* Annapolis, Maryland: Naval Institute Press, 2001.

Skaggs, Davis Curtis. *Oliver Hazard Perry.* Annapolis, Maryland: Naval Institute Press, 2006.

Stensrud, Rockwell. *Newport: A Lively Experiment, 1639-1969.* Newport, Rhode Island: The Redwood Library and Athenaeum, 2006.

Sterling, John, et al., *Newport, Rhode Island Colonial Burial Grounds* Hope, Rhode Island: Rhode Island Genealogical Society, 2009, xxiii.

Tiffany, Nelson Otis. *The Tiffanys of America: A History and Genealogy.* Self- published, 1901.

Veit, Richard F, and Mark Nonestied. *New Jersey Cemeteries and Tombstones: History in the Landscape.* New Brunswick, New Jersey: Rivergate Books, 2008.

Viola, Herman J. *The Indian Legacy of Charles Bird King.* Washington,
D.C.: Smithsonian Institution Press, 1976.

Wilson, Robert. *The Explorer King: Adventure, Science, and the Great
Diamond Hoax-Clarence King in the Old West.* New York:
Scribner, 2006.

Yarnall, James. *Newport through its Architecture: A History of Styles
from Postmedieval to Postmodern.* Hanover, New Hampshire: University Press of New England, 2005

NEWSPAPERS

The Berkshire Eagle
Boston Evening Transcript
The Boston Globe
The Boston Post
Brattleboro Reformer
The Brooklyn Daily Eagle
Brownsville Herald
Colorado Springs Gazette
Fall River Daily Evening News
The Fall River Daily Herald
Newport Mercury
Newport Daily News
Newport Mercury and Weekly News
Newport This Week
The New York Times
New York Tribune
The Providence Journal
The Washington Post

WEBSITES

Ancestry
Http://ancestry.com

Find A Grave
Http://findagrave.com

Newport History: Journal of the Newport Historical Society
Http://digitalcommons.salve.edu/newporthistory

Database of Classical Scholars, Rutgers School of Arts and Sciences
Http://dbcs.rutgers.edu

Jeffrey Staats
Http://jeffreystaatsarchitect.com

Collection of the Redwood Library and Athenaeum
Https://redwoodlibrary.pastperfectonline.com

Island Cemetery, Newport
Http://islandcemeterynewport.com

Belmont Chapel
Http://belmontchapelfoundation.org

City of Newport Property Records
Https://i2l.uslandrecords.com/RI/Newport

Rhode Island Historical Cemeteries
Http://rihistoriccemeteries.org/webdatabase

Wikipedia
Https://www.wikipedia.org

Wikimapia
Http://www.wikimapia.org

Applications for inclusion in National Register of Historic
Places for Common Burying Ground/Island Cemetery; Southern
Thames Historic District; Kay Street - Catherine Street – Old
Beach Road Historic District can be found at
Https://preservation.ri.gov/sites/g/files

Index

www.ingramcontent.com/pod-product-compliance
Lightning Source LLC
Chambersburg PA
CBHW060916120626
46553CB00001B/343